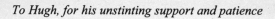

To Hugh, for his unstinting support and patience

D0318554

Susan Osborne

The Pocket Essential

FEMINISM

LEARNING
RESOURCES
CENTRE

WITHDRAWN

www.pocketessentials.com

First published in Great Britain 2001 by Pocket Essentials, 18 Coleswood Road,
Harpenden, Herts, AL5 1EQ

Distributed in the USA by Trafalgar Square Publishing, PO Box 257, Howe Hill
Road, North Pomfret, Vermont 05053

A CIP catalogue record for this book is available from the British Library.

ISBN 1-903047-51-X

9 8 7 6 5 4 3 2 1

Book typeset by Pdunk
Printed and bound by Cox & Wyman

CONTENTS

1. Feminism: A Short History

Introduction

Together with sex, drugs and rock 'n' roll, feminism sprang into life in the late sixties and seventies attracting acres of media attention and generating a tremendous energy that translated into real change in many women's lives. But the roots of 'women's liberation', as it came to be known at that time, can be traced back to the late eighteenth century when the revolutionary zeal in France began to influence writers such as Mary Wollstonecraft whose *Vindication of the Rights of Women* is seen as the foundation of modern feminism. It's been a long, slow haul with many fits and starts but the achievements of the last two hundred years have revolutionised the lives of women. Some commentators have suggested that we now live in a post-feminist world where women have achieved equality with men and so there is no longer a need for a women's movement. This seems a little hard to swallow given that, even in the Western world where campaigns for equality have been strongest, the average wage for women is still less than average male earnings. Despite some notable advances for women in the political arena, there has still been no serious female contender for the American Presidency or for the premiership of many other countries. Maybe when half the world's leaders are women we can say that feminism's work is over.

Feminism has become a huge area of study since the resurgence of the women's movement in the sixties. Conferences, dissertations, debates and websites abound on the subject. In universities throughout the world academics are teaching, researching and contributing to the explosion in feminist literature which hit the bookshelves in the late twentieth century and continues to do so. It can be hard to find your way through the maze of information on offer. This book tries to make the task a little simpler by tracing the path of a movement that has taken many twists and turns since its beginning. Its aim is to give an overview of feminism, a straightforward 'what happened when', backed up by short summaries of some key texts and potted biographies of key figures, rather than a detailed analysis which can be safely left to the academics. Geographically, the book concentrates on British and American feminism. To take things much beyond that would be outside the scope of such a slim volume.

So, where do we start? Coming up with some sort of definition might help.

What is Feminism?

Try searching the Internet and you will come up with pages of definitions, many subtly different. The *Oxford Concise Dictionary of Politics* begins:

> Feminism is a way of looking at the world, which women occupy from the perspective of women. It has as its central focus the concept of patriarchy, which can be described as a system of male authority, which oppresses women through its social, political and economic institutions.

And then carries on in a similar vein for several paragraphs. *Chambers Dictionary* puts it more simply as the 'advocacy of women's rights, or of the movement for the advancement and emancipation of women' and that's the one we'll be sticking with, although Rebecca West certainly has the edge on both of these with her comment that:

> I myself have never been able to find out precisely what feminism is: I only know that people call me a feminist whenever I express sentiments that differentiate me from a doormat...

When did it all begin?

The origins of the women's movement in the Western world can be traced back to the French Revolution which began in 1789. That's not to say that women had not stood up for themselves before that or that there were no women of any note. Boadicea, Elizabeth I (1533 - 1603), Empress Catherine the Great of Russia (1729 - 96) and Joan of Arc (1412 - 31) all spring to mind but these are notable exceptions and, rather like Margaret Thatcher, sisterhood did not seem to be on their agenda.

There were quieter examples of women who not only made their own way in the world but also protested against the inequalities between the sexes. Christine de Pizan (1364 - 1430) was a Venetian writer whose book *Treasures of the City of Ladies*, a collection of snippets of advice to women, is still quoted today. Pizan refused to accept the male certainties that women were both inherently weaker than men and more likely to fall into evil ways. Three centuries later, Mary Astell (1666 - 1731) wrote *Reflections on Marriage*, perhaps the earliest English feminist text. Astell wrote not only about the inequality between men and women in marriage but also about the lack of educational opportunities for women.

Meanwhile, Aphra Behn (1640 - 1689) managed to establish herself as the first English woman playwright, exploring themes such as the consequences of arranged and ill-matched marriages. However, such women were few and far between and the status quo remained largely unchallenged.

There was little choice for women in how they led their lives. For the gentry, marriage, the convent or scratching a living as a governess were just about the only options. Although Aphra Behn was the first in a long and honourable tradition of women writers, few women were able to rely on this for their living.

For the less well off, before industrialisation, men and women worked together on the farm or in the workshop. Both the work women did and the amount they were paid differed from men. With the spread of industrialisation came a more formalised separation between 'men's work' and 'women's work'. Whatever their economic and social background, there was no active role for women in public life and by the late eighteenth century, some women were beginning to chafe against such restriction.

The French Revolution, Olympe de Gouges and Mary Wollstonecraft

The demand for women's rights that began to be voiced in the late eighteenth century forms the basis of modern feminism. Women's voices were first raised in unison during the French Revolution in which many of them took an active part. Citoyennes, Republicaines, Révolutionnaires (Revolutionary Republican Women Citizens) called for the right for women to vote and to hold senior civilian and military posts in the new Republic. Having fought along-side men, women were bitterly disappointed when the revolutionaries' *Declaration of the Rights of Man and the Citizen* (1789) explicitly denied equality with their male *compadres*. Olympe de Gouge replied in 1791 with her *Declaration of the Rights of Women* calling for equal rights with men. De Gouges, a member of the royalist Girondin faction, persisted in her demands and was sent to the guillotine in 1793 during the Jacobin Terror (see Key Figures and Texts).

Across the Channel, Mary Wollstonecraft enthusiastically debated the events in France with her radical friends. A keen supporter of the French revolutionaries, Wollstonecraft's *A Vindication of the Rights of Man* (1790) was her passionate reply to Edmund Burke's attack on the Revolution, *Reflections on the Revolution in France* (1790). Like de Gouges, Wollstonecraft found herself deeply frustrated by the revolutionaries' neglect of women's rights. Her most famous work, *A Vindication of the Rights of Women*, was written in 1792, the year after De Gouges' *Declaration*. Although nineteenth century feminists distanced themselves from Wollstonecraft, unwilling to be associated with her outspoken opinions on sexuality and the scandal of her illegitimate daughter, the *Vindication* is now seen as the foundation stone upon which modern feminism was built. It is a passionate critique of both the education available to women and the assumptions surrounding marriage and family life. Claiming that the financial dependence of women on their husbands amounted to little more than 'legalised prostitution', Wollstonecraft demanded that women be recognised as citizens in their own right with equality of access to both education and employment (see Key Figures and Texts).

Coming at the same question from an entirely different angle, Hannah More's pamphlet, *Strictures on the Modern System of Female Education* (1799), called for an educational system tailored to enable women to be moral guardians to their children, carry out their philanthropic duties and lay the foundations for a marriage based on friendship. The antithesis of Wollstonecraft in both her life and her work, More's links with evangelical philanthropy, coupled with her conservatism, meant that her views were far more likely to be listened to by a society made jittery by events in France.

Although she seems an unlikely feminist, with her acceptance of the sexual hierarchy, Hannah More made a significant contribution to the movement. As society became more industrialised, divisions between men and women became more pronounced. In the newly expanding middle classes, material conditions improved but women still found themselves confined to the domestic sphere and expected to find fulfilment in their role as moral educators of the next generation. More capitalised on this idea by taking it outside the home and helping to establish a role for women which would later enable nineteenth century feminists like Josephine Butler to extend the boundaries of moral education into campaigning for women's rights (see Key Figures).

As writers, both Wollstonecraft and More were part of a growing number of women in the eighteenth century who saw literature as a viable profession. Not only did it offer educated women a small measure of financial independence, it also provided a way of drawing attention to the difficulties faced by women. Novelists such as Mary Hays, Fanny Burney, Maria Edgeworth and, later, Jane Austen debated what became known as the 'Woman Question' in their novels. They addressed concerns about marriage, motherhood and family life, sometimes extending the debate to include such difficult issues as rape and prostitution (see Key Texts).

William Thompson's Appeal and the sad story of Caroline Norton.

In the bloody aftermath of the French Revolution, Britain was in no mood for anything but conservatism. This together with the whiff of scandal surrounding Mary Wollstonecraft's reputation, confirmed for many by the *Memoirs* (1798) written by her husband William Godwin, meant that her ideas were not openly discussed for some time.

Women continued to establish some sort of civic role for themselves by raising money during the Napoleonic Wars with France but little else was done to further their emancipation.

In the 1820s there was a renewal of interest in social, parliamentary and legal reform. William Thompson's *Appeal Of One-Half of the Human Race, Women, Against the Pretensions of the Other Half, Men, to retain them in Political and thence in Civil and Domestic Slavery* (1825) put forward radical demands for female emancipation in reply to James Mill's *Article on Government*. Thompson refuted Mill's arguments against universal enfranchisement, comparing the situation of women to the slavery that the recently formed abolitionist movement was attempting to eradicate in America. Claiming to be a mouthpiece for Anna Wheeler, a fellow member of the Owenite co-operative movement, Thompson's *Appeal* was an impassioned plea for reform and equality (see Key Figures and Texts)

Thompson's indictment of marriage is graphically illustrated by the sad story of Caroline Norton. Trapped in a violent marriage, Norton found herself barred from her own house after a short absence. At this time, women had virtually no legal standing once they were married. Any property that they owned, including income from that property, passed into the hands of their husband on marriage. They were unable to enter into legal contracts of any kind and had no rights over their children. Even rape was legal within marriage. For many years Norton was denied access to her three young sons. Desperate, she set about trying to change the law, writing and distributing pamphlets about her situation. Although she met with no success, her book *English Laws for Women* (1854), brought the question of legal reform for women into the forefront of the public arena. Some progress in marital law was made with the Divorce Act of 1857 which made it easier for women to leave hellish marriages, but the sexual double standard was enshrined by making it possible for a man to divorce a woman on grounds of adultery, while women had to prove that men were also cruel, bigamous or incestuous. Despite her appalling treatment by her husband, Norton continued to support the idea of male superiority, refusing to countenance the idea of women's rights as a part of her appeal for legal reform (see Key Texts).

How the movement for the abolition of slavery became a potent force for feminism

The debate sparked by Thompson and Mill with their opposing arguments on enfranchisement attracted a good deal of attention from those interested in social reform including the writer, Harriet Martineau. Under a male pseudonym, she wrote on a wide range of subjects including education, marriage laws, prostitution and health, linking these issues with the oppression of women but prudently kept her distance from the passionate appeals of both Thompson and Wollstonecraft.

In 1834, the year after the founding of the American Anti-Slavery Society, Martineau visited America where she met activists in the abolitionist movement such as Lucretia Mott (see Key Figures) and the Grimke sisters. In America, all-women abolitionist groups such as the Philadelphia Female Anti-Slavery Society founded by Mott, were becoming involved in debates on women's rights.

Throughout the 1830s and 1840s the links between the abolitionists and feminism grew stronger. In 1840 the World Anti-Slavery Convention was held in London. Not only were women delegates not allowed to take part in the debate; they were forced to suffer the indignity of listening to the proceedings from behind a curtain. For some, including Lucretia Mott and her colleague, Elizabeth Cady Stanton both of whom were to become prominent in the founding of the American women's movement, this was a turning point. After the Convention, many of the American abolitionists toured Britain. Useful links were forged between delegates such as Mott and Stanton and the women who came to hear them speak. Women involved in the abolitionist cause could hardly fail to see the similarities between themselves and the slaves they were trying to emancipate.

For many women, two factors were essential to achieve their own emancipation - equality of education and enfranchisement. Only with equal opportunities in education could women hope to work towards equality in employment with men and attain financial independence. Only with the vote would they have their say in policymaking. Alongside these two major areas, activists like Josephine Butler, another veteran of the abolition movement, continued their work for women's rights by campaigning against such oppressive laws as the Contagious Diseases Act which had virtually legalised brothels in certain towns (see Key Figures).

Education opens doors

Whilst women had been assigned the role of 'moral educators' in the home, destined to keep the next generation on the straight and narrow, opportunities for their own education were minimal. In the eighteenth century women were likely to be educated at home. Hannah More's *Strictures on the Modern System of Female Education* (1799) had been influential in raising the subject of education for women and by the middle of the nineteenth century there was a good deal of debate on the issue. In 1854 Barbara Bodichon and Bessie Parkes established what would later become known as the Langham Place Circle to debate educational and legal issues for women. They set up *The English Woman's Journal* as a platform for that debate, attracting many feminists to the circle including Adelaide

Proctor and Jessie Boucheret who set up the Society for Promoting the Employment of Women.

Feminists mounted campaigns for improvements in opportunities in higher education. Bodichon worked alongside Josephine Butler to persuade Cambridge University to offer more opportunities for women students resulting in the provision of lectures for women and the eventual establishment of Newnham College. Emily Davies's campaign for equal educational opportunities ultimately succeeded in the establishment of Girton College, Cambridge in 1873. Although many activists such as Butler felt that educational opportunities should be improved for women, Davies was one of the few who insisted that they should be equal and it was thanks to her that women were admitted to the University of London in 1878. The previous year another victory had been gained when Elizabeth Garrett Anderson succeeded in her battle to gain the right for women to register as physicians.

The big issue - the battle for the enfranchisement of women

From the mid-nineteenth century the battle for the vote occupied the women's movement on both sides of the Atlantic. For both American and British women it was a long, hard and often bitter fight. The American Congress pipped Parliament to the post by awarding women the vote in 1920. Whilst British women over thirty were enfranchised in 1917, it was not until 1928 that equal voting rights with men were achieved.

The American suffrage movement

The American women's movement had in effect been established in 1848 with the Seneca Falls women's rights convention organised by Lucretia Mott (see Key Figures) and Elizabeth Cady Stanton. After their exclusion from the debates that took place at the 1840 Anti-Slavery Convention in London solely because of their gender, the American suffragists turned their attention to women's rights.

The Seneca Falls convention issued a *Declaration of Sentiments* echoing the language of the *Declaration of Independence*, in its statement that 'all men and women are created equal...' It attracted a good deal of press attention, much of it hostile. Mott, Stanton, Susan B. Anthony (see Key Figures) and many others lectured throughout America, campaigning on such issues as married women's right to own property, equal rights to education, employment and the vote. After spending five months gathering signatures for a petition, Stanton appealed to the New York Legislature against a law compelling employers to pay women's wages to their husbands. Her hard work paid off - by the mid-1850s many State legislatures were sympathetic to her appeals and by 1860 fourteen states had passed reforms.

American female suffragists called off their campaigns during the Civil War, siding with the Union cause in support of the emancipation of slaves. When the war ended, efforts were made to link the enfranchisement of freed slaves with votes for women. The failure of this initiative provoked much bitterness. The movement split in 1869 when Lucy Stone (see Key Figures) chose to support both the Fourteenth Amendment, which secured equal legal rights for all US born citizens but introduced the word 'male' with regard to voting rights, and the Fifteenth Amendment, which enfranchised black men but did not extend the vote to women. Anthony and Stanton's National Woman Suffrage Association continued their more militant campaign for a full constitutional amendment on women's suffrage whilst Stone's American Woman Suffrage Association campaigned for the vote on a state by state basis. The two factions were reconciled in 1890. American women finally won the right to vote when Congress adopted the Nineteenth Amendment in 1920.

The British suffrage campaign and the emergence of the 'new woman'

The British women's suffrage campaign spanned sixty-one years from 1867, when the first National Societies for Women's Suffrage were set up in Manchester and London, to 1928 when full voting rights for women were finally secured by the Equal Franchise Act.

The influential philosopher, John Stuart Mill was a founding member of the London branch of National Societies for Women's Suffrage. Mill's views had been heavily influenced by his relationship with Harriet Taylor with whom he had written many articles on women's rights. He had become a champion of women's suffrage and in his book *The Subjection of Women* (1869) argued that enfranchisement was the key to freedom for women. In 1865 Mill had been elected to Parliament and had attempted to add an amendment on women's suffrage to the 1867 Reform Act (see Key Figures and Texts).

Under Mill's leadership the London branch emphasised the importance of feminine decorum but the Manchester approach was very different. It was led by Lydia Becker who travelled the region speaking on suffrage and reporting her progress through the *Women's Suffrage Journal*, which she edited from 1870 until her death in 1881. In it she pointed to the importance of legal and political reform citing cases of brutality and drawing explicit parallels between black slaves and women. The *Journal* consistently attacked the laws on married women's property including the 1870 Married Women's Property Act which failed to safeguard inherited property and income for women's own use. It was not until the 1882 Married Women's Property Act that married women's property was finally secured for their own use.

By the 1890s the question of women's rights had finally come to the fore. As a new generation became involved in the campaign there was a good deal of debate on the 'new woman'. Mary Wollstonecraft was rehabilitated and even members of the old guard embraced her. The meaning of marriage, the sexual double standard and many other aspects of the 'new woman' became a feature of fiction such as Olive Schreiner's *The Story of an African Farm* (1883), Sarah Grand's *Heavenly Twins* (1893) and Thomas Hardy's *Jude the Obscure* (1895).

Over time, two strands had emerged in the campaign for women's suffrage in Britain. The moderate strand was led by Millicent Garrett Fawcett (see Key Figures), a fervent supporter of John Stuart Mill, who had served on the Married Women's Property Commission. She became an active member of the London Suffrage Committee in

1868, leading the National Union of Women's Suffrage Societies from 1897. The other more militant and better-known strand was led by Emmeline Pankhurst with the help of her daughter Christabel (see Key Figures).

In 1903 Emmeline Pankhurst set up the Women's Social and Political Union, attracting women from all walks of life including teachers, clerks, dressmakers and textile workers. Millicent Garrett Fawcett's support of Bryant and May, a company in which she was a shareholder, in the 1889 'match girl' strike for better pay and conditions had raised questions for the women's movement. Activists such as Eva Gore Booth began to highlight problems facing working class women. Whereas the movement had previously been almost exclusively middle class, feminists, as they were now coming to be known, began to understand the diversity of women and of the problems that they faced. The 1880s and 1890s saw a proliferation of organisations concerned with women's labour such as the Women's Trade Union League and the Women's Co-operative Guild. For these organisations, suffrage took a back seat to women's employment issues.

The move towards militancy in the suffrage movement began in 1905 with the arrest of Annie Kenney and Christabel Pankhurst after they interrupted a Liberal election meeting, demanding to know the party's stance on votes for women. When the militants stepped up their campaigns, with such actions as chaining themselves to the Ladies Gallery in Parliament in 1908, the moderates disassociated themselves. The militants succeeded in capturing public attention, provoking a good deal of hostility as well as support. Organisations such as the Women's

Anti-Suffrage League were established and suffragists were cruelly lampooned by the press.

In 1911, Prime Minister Asquith agreed that a bill would be proposed giving propertied women the vote in return for a moratorium on demonstrations at the Coronation of the new King. When the bill was blocked, the suffragists' anger was unleashed on the windows of the Home Office, the Board of Trade, the Treasury and the National Liberal Club. All over the West End, more windows were smashed and there were many arrests. Once in jail, the suffragists went on hunger strike and were subjected to the pain and indignity of forced feeding, resulting in a public outcry. The government's response was to introduce a 'Cat and Mouse' Act whereby women were released when their health began to fail, only to be re-arrested when they were sufficiently well.

When war broke out in 1914, the campaign was called to a halt. Many women became involved in the war effort, some working as voluntary nursing assistants at the Front, movingly described by Vera Brittain in her book, *Testament of Youth*. The 1917 Representation of the People Act gave women over thirty the vote in acknowledgement of their contribution to the war effort.

The years between the wars

Although many women had become involved in war work, much of it had been voluntary and did little to advance employment opportunities after the war. Those women who had found jobs in areas of work previously done by men found themselves out of a job once the war was over. There was still much to be done in the battle for equal rights.

In 1919 the National Union of Women's Suffrage Societies became the National Union of Societies for Equal Citizenship (NUSEC) under the leadership of Eleanor Rathbone (see Key Figures). Its declared aim was 'to obtain all such reforms as are necessary to secure real equality of liberties, status and opportunities between men and women'. The NUSEC set out a six point programme which consisted of equal voting rights with men; an equal moral standard; the promotion of women candidates as MPs; equal pay for equal work and equal employment opportunities; widows' pensions and equal guardianship, and support of the League of Nations, which had been set up after the First World War. Under Eleanor Rathbone's leadership the organisation turned its attentions towards educating women for citizenship.

The first woman MP to be elected to the House of Commons took her seat in Parliament in 1919. As an American millionairess, Nancy Astor could hardly be described as a feminist pioneer but she was amenable to acting as a spokeswoman on feminist issues in the House.

Other areas of debate were opening up. Women's sexuality and the contentious issue of birth control began to be debated more openly by feminists such as Dora Russell. The magazine *Time and Tide*, set up in 1920 by Lady Margaret Rhondda, published many articles on these and other feminist issues.

Although the twenties may have seemed quiet after the militant campaigns before the War, significant advances were achieved. In 1920 Oxford University admitted women to degrees. The 1923 Matrimonial Causes Act allowed women to sue for divorce on the basis of adultery and in the same year, the Guardianship of Infants Act gave divorced women the right to custody of their children. In 1924 Ellen Wilkinson was elected the first woman Labour MP, giving working class women a voice in Parliament. The crowning glory was, of course, the granting of full enfranchisement to women through the Equal Enfranchisement Act of 1928. With the attainment of full suffrage the feminist emphasis shifted to welfare exemplified by Eleanor Rathbone's work on the proposal of a family allowance to be paid directly to mothers.

As the Depression began to loom in the late twenties, opportunities for advances in women's rights began to close down. Little more would be achieved until after the Second World War.

The Second World War and its legacy

Just as they had in the war of 1914-1918, women stepped into men's jobs during the Second World War. On both sides of the Atlantic women took on engineering work, earning the affectionate nickname of Rosie the Riveter in the United States. In Britain, the marriage bar enforced in teaching and the civil service in 1920 was suspended. It would be abolished in 1944 but women civil servants would have to wait until 1946 before they could continue in their jobs after marriage. As in the First World War, pay and conditions did not match what had been on offer to men. Concern was such that an Equal Pay Campaign Committee was set up in 1943 headed by the MPs

Edith Summerskill and Mavis Tate. Small advances were made in the years immediately after the War such as the admittance of women to the police force in 1945 but equal pay remained an issue. Although it was introduced for teachers in 1952 and for civil servants in 1954, it would be many years before more general legislation would be brought in.

On the whole, the independence, which many women had relished, slipped away when men returned from the war looking for work. In the fifties, the emphasis was very firmly on the joys of marriage and motherhood. Although some women continued to work, the cosy image of the stay-at-home wife and mother as the lynchpin of a stable household was encouraged as the ideal.

It was not until the late 50s and early 60s that the 'woman question' bounced back on to the agenda. Women's pages began to appear in respectable broadsheets such as *The Times* and *The Guardian*. They focussed on childcare, problems facing women at work and debated the meaning of equality between the sexes. *Woman's Hour*, a new BBC radio programme, discussed similar questions. With the publication of Simone de Beauvoir's *The Second Sex*, which appeared in translation in 1954, and Betty Friedan's *The Feminine Mystique*, published in 1963, the debate became intense (see Key Figures and Texts).

The birth of Women's Liberation

Often called the 'second wave', the first wave being the suffragists, women's liberation grew into a vibrant, sprawling movement that eventually seemed to encompass as many factions as there were women in it. Just as the militant suffragists had found themselves in the spotlight, the second wave of feminists attracted a good deal of media attention not to mention derision in some quarters. Feminists were regarded with suspicion and never more so than when they attended the consciousness-raising groups that were popular in both Britain and the United States. For many feminists these discussion groups, which aimed to help women understand the nature of their oppression, were the core of the movement.

America

The Feminine Mystique with its analysis of discontent amongst middle class, educated American women, stripped away the myth of the happy housewife content with her role as creator of a domestic haven for her husband and children, and exposed the misery and frustration which lay beneath. On both sides of the Atlantic, women read the book with grateful recognition.

In 1966 Friedan helped set up NOW, the National Organisation of Women, to debate issues of sex discrimination. With a wide range of contacts both in the media and in political lobbies, NOW began vociferous campaigning, picketing the Equal Employment Opportunity Commission, sending angry telegrams to Washington, filing a complaint against the New York Times for its sex-segregated job advertisements, to name but a few of its initiatives.

To a certain extent, the American women's liberation movement sprang out of the wave of anti-Vietnam War protests that swept through college campuses in the sixties.

Although politically active in the protests women were still expected to get on with making the coffee. When, in 1967, a student conference dropped the feminist resolution from their agenda, women had had enough. They had their own issues to protest and in the following year the women's liberation movement erupted into life. At the Miss America contest in 1968 a group of protesters known as the Redstockings put on non-stop street theatre outside the contest hall to show how women were degraded by the competition. The performance culminated in the crowning of a sheep. Protestors threw objects that they felt symbolised their oppression into the Freedom Trash Can, including wire-cupped bras. Although the Freedom Trash Can was never burnt, the media were quick to construct the myth of bra-burning that was forever linked with women's liberation.

In 1970 NOW called for a Women's Strike to mark the fiftieth anniversary of female suffrage. The level of support and media attention took the organisers by surprise. Women's liberation had become a major issue.

Britain

In 1966 *The New Left Review* published an essay by Juliet Mitchell called 'Women: The Longest Revolution' in which she shifted the feminist debate away from emancipation towards 'liberation' from the many constraints that oppressed women. A quiet beginning for British women's liberation but two years later legislation was passed which enabled women to obtain an abortion, providing two doctors agreed that pregnancy would be detrimental to mental or physical health. In 1968, the fiftieth anniversary of the first step towards female suffrage was taken seriously enough for the BBC to devote a day to programmes and debates on women's issues.

In 1970, this quiet debate exploded in a burst of energy with a theatrical demonstration against the Miss World beauty competition which was televised from London. Women protestors ran onto the stage, mooing like cows and wearing placards bearing titles such as Miss-conception, Miss-treated, Miss-placed and Miss-judged. Flour-bombs, stink-bombs and smoke-bombs were let off whilst Bob Hope and a bewildered panel of judges ran away, followed by a line of tearful beauties. Five women were arrested in a protest of which the Pankhursts would surely have been proud.

The demonstrations at both the 1968 Miss America and the 1970 Miss World contests indicated a concern for the way in which women were portrayed as objects which feminists found both degrading and oppressive. The debate was to be taken further by writers such as Susie Orbach in *Fat is a Feminist Issue*, published in 1978, and, many years later, Naomi Wolf in *The Beauty Myth* (see Key Texts).

The first national Women's Conference was held at Ruskin College, Oxford in 1970. The following demands were put forward - equal pay, equal education and employment opportunities, twenty-four hour nurseries, free contraception and abortion on demand. To make their point, feminists paraded their demands on banners through the streets, shouting them out as they marched. The emphasis was on choice for women. Later three more demands were added - legal and financial independence, freedom for women to express their sexuality and an end to the oppression of lesbians.

History became very important in British feminism. Both Juliet Mitchell and Sheila Rowbotham were active in this area. Rowbotham's *Hidden from History* emphasised the importance of historical context in understanding women's oppression (see Key Texts). The magazine *Spare Rib* also played a part in placing the movement within its context, publishing articles on the suffragists but also interviewing feminists such as Dora Russell and Mary Stott who had been active earlier in the twentieth century.

Diversity within the movement

In contrast to nineteenth century feminism which was largely united around the cause of suffrage, the women's liberation movement was extraordinarily diverse. In the US a women's liberation directory was set up which listed everything from women's karate classes to followers of the Goddess. Separate groups addressing particular issues sprang up - Black Women's Liberation activists protested against racial oppression and stereotypes which applied to black women whilst Lesbian Liberation emphasised lesbian oppression. Factions within the movement are far too numerous to mention but broadly it split in to three major ideologies:

Radical feminists defined the problem as one of patriarchy in which male domination in all areas of life had resulted in wholesale oppression of women. This faction mounted women-only campaigns which focussed on the effects of male violence, rape and pornography. In the United

States, Andrea Dworkin still continues her battle against pornography (see Key Figures).

Marxist Feminists linked male domination with class exploitation, arguing that equal rights for men and women wouldn't improve the lot of poor women.

Liberal feminists placed the emphasis on change from within society rather than revolution by putting forward positive role models for girls, establishing equality in their own relationships and lobbying parliament for legislation on equal rights.

There were, however, two issues on which the majority of feminists could agree.

The two big issues - abortion and equal pay

Abortion - the right to choose

The legalisation of abortion was a major issue for the feminist movement. Many on both sides of the Atlantic campaigned for abortion on demand both as a means of eradicating the often tragic results of back street abortions and to give women the right to choose what happened to their bodies. Whilst in Britain, legalised abortion passed comparatively quietly onto the statute book in 1968, the famous Roe v. Wade Supreme Court decision of 1973 which in effect gave women the right to choose to have an abortion, provoked outrage in the United States. Abortion remains a hugely controversial issue in the States. Militant anti-abortion campaigners routinely harass doctors who practise abortion - some have been murdered at the hands of extremists. In Britain, abortion on demand remained an issue, although, over time, the required assessment by two doctors as to the effect of pregnancy on a woman's health became something of a formality.

Equal Pay for equal work

In 1963 the Equal Pay Act had been passed in the United States backed up by legislation in the following year on equal opportunity. Although an Equal Rights Amendment had first been introduced in 1923 by Alice Paul, it has still not been ratified by all the states. In the second wave of feminism, NOW put a good deal of effort in to trying to get this through so that equal pay and equal opportunity would be enshrined in the American Constitution.

It was not until 1975 that sex discrimination on both pay and employment opportunities was outlawed in Britain. In 1976, the Equal Opportunities Commission was set up to work to end sex discrimination, promote equal opportunities for men and women, and review and suggest amendments to the legislation.

Both the American Equal Employment Opportunities Commission and the British Equal Opportunities Commission are still kept very busy.

In 1979, the British elected Margaret Thatcher as their first woman Prime Minister although sisterhood was the last thing on her mind.

Post-feminism or the Third Wave?

A wave of conservatism swept through the Western world in the eighties, spearheaded by Margaret Thatcher and Ronald Reagan. Feminism quietened down although the Greenham Women set up camp around the perimeter fence of the US Air Force base at Greenham Common in 1981 to protest against the siting of Cruise missiles on British soil. They were a solid reminder that there was still a movement out there (see Key Figures).

There was much talk of a post-feminist world in which women had achieved equal rights and therefore no longer needed a movement to campaign for change. Feminists had been derided and caricatured to such an extent by the media that many women disassociated themselves from the movement by prefacing their criticism of a society still dominated by men with the phrase 'I'm not a feminist but…'.

In the early nineties young feminist writers, such as Naomi Wolf, Katie Roiphe, and Susan Faludi (see Key Figures), began to be recognised in the States as representatives of a new generation of feminists. The highly publicised accusations of sexual harassment made by Anita Hill against Clarence Thomas, then a Supreme Court nominee, put women's issues back on the agenda in 1991. In 1995 the UN Fourth World Conference on Women, held in Beijing, highlighted the need for recognition of women's issues.

A new movement began to emerge in the States calling themselves the Third Wave. A Third Wave Foundation was set up in 1996 to promote such issues as social security reform, particularly important to women who are in and out of the work force, voter registration and women's health. The Foundation offered scholarships and fees to help young women campaign against inequalities faced by women either because of their gender or because of other forms of oppression based on race, creed, sexual orientation or poverty.

If the nineteenth century campaign for suffrage was the first wave of feminism and the demands for equal rights voiced by the women's liberation movement of the 1960s and 70s was the second, what are the aims of the third wave?

What's happening now?

Many modern feminists, whilst acknowledging the debt they owe to the women's liberation movement, feel that things have moved on. There are better employment opportunities, legislation in place to enforce equal pay in most Western countries and childcare is on the agenda of most governments. The areas of debate in modern feminism are many and varied but several issues stand out above the others.

The backlash debate

In 1991 Susan Faludi published her influential book *Backlash* in which she explored ways in which the advances made as a result of the second wave of feminism were being undermined in the media (see Key Texts). Faludi sparked off a debate that is still running. Naomi Wolf gave the debate a different slant in *Fire with Fire* (1993) by suggesting that it was time for women to cast aside their fears and stand up for what they wanted. In 1999 Germaine Greer, the redoubtable second wave feminist, called for women to 'get angry again' in her book *The Whole Woman*, taking young women to task for assuming that the battle had been won.

Political representation

Women are still woefully under-represented in politics. In 1985, twenty-five women got together in America to set up a fundraising organisation to raise money to help pro-choice Democratic women candidates. They called their organisation Emily's List and it now boasts more than 65,000 donors. A British Emily's list followed in 1993. The 1997 general election saw a something of a readjustment of the gender balance in the British Parliament with an influx of Labour women MPs as a result of the party's landslide victory. However, out of a total of 659 seats in the House of Commons, only 120 were held by women in November 2000 and many of them were unhappy with the family-unfriendly way that Parliament operates.

Sexual Harassment

Sexual harassment came to the fore as a result of the Anita Hill/Clarence Thomas debacle and remains an important issue on the feminist agenda despite the use of sex discrimination legislation aimed at eliminating it from the workplace. Away from work the debate encompasses such issues as women's right to dress how they wish whether men consider that to be provocative or not. Feminists argue that it's men's responsibility to keep their libidos under control.

Body Image

The emphasis upon the way women look and the way that they are portrayed in magazines, film and television has been on the feminist agenda since the beginning of the second wave. Whilst beauty contests may now be seen as a thing of the past, body image is still a major issue for feminists. Many commentators such as Naomi Wolf argue that the idealised images of youthful, slender beauty that dominate film, television and advertising hoardings damage many women's self-esteem resulting in eating disorders, depression and poor self-image (see Key Texts)

Inclusivity

The third wave aims to move away from the domination of feminism by white middle class women to a more inclusive movement which addresses inequalities aggravated by attitudes toward racial minorities, sexual orientation and physical disablement. Attitudes towards men have softened providing they play their part in aiming for a more egalitarian society.

So, what has been achieved over the last two hundred years?

Mary Wollstonecraft would surely be delighted with many of the advances made since the publication of *A Vindication of Woman's Rights* in 1792. Women throughout the world have been enfranchised. They have equal access to education and equal employment, with legislation in place to protect these rights in many countries. In the Western world women's sexuality is openly recognised and the sexual double standard has largely been whittled away. Many women are financially independent and in charge of their own lives.

However there is still much to do. Women are far from equally represented in political organisations. Although there have been several women premiers such as Indira Gandhi, Golda Meir and Margaret Thatcher, they are still comparatively rare. Young women often excel in education, but there are few women in senior management or executive positions. Equal pay for equal work is enshrined in the law but women are still often to be found in the lowest paid jobs. Women still put in more hours working in the home than their male partners even if they are working full time themselves and sometimes earning more.

We may have come a long way but it ain't over yet.

2. Key Feminist Texts

Listed below are sixteen key texts which track the evolution of feminism from Olympe de Gouges' *Declaration of the Rights of Women* in 1791 to *Backlash,* Susan Faludi's angry yet meticulously researched attack on those who have sought to undermine modern women's achievements. The two hundred years between these two are peppered with spirited and cogently argued texts - this list documents a small but significant selection.

Declaration of the Rights of Women and of the Citizen by Olympe de Gouges (1791)

Olympe de Gouges' *Declaration* heavily influenced Mary Wollstonecraft's *A Vindication of the Rights of Women*, and can perhaps be seen as the cornerstone of Western feminism. It was written out of a deep sense of disappointment and betrayal at the failure of the French revolutionaries to address the rights of women in their *Declaration of the Rights of Man and the Citizen* (1789). De Gouges argued that women may not be the same as men but they are equal. Urging women to wake up to their continuing enslavement, she launched an attack on marriage as a tool of oppression and drafted a new 'social contract between man and woman' based on equality in every sphere including parenthood. She also pressed for men to be accountable for the children they fathered outside marriage. Sadly, de Gouges paid for her truly revolutionary zeal with her life.

A Vindication of the Rights of Women by Mary Wollestonecraft (1792)

Widely regarded as the text, which triggered the beginning of the Anglo/American feminist movement, *A Vindication of the Rights of Women* followed on from *A Vindication of the Rights of Man* (1790), Wollstonecraft's defence of the French revolution. When it became clear that the French had failed to address the rights of women Wollstonecraft wrote this powerful critique both of women's education and the assumptions surrounding marriage and family life. Whilst she argued that women are different from men, she did not see that such a difference should bar them from entering any sphere they chose or result in a hierarchy with men at the top. She argued that women's financial dependence coupled with the sexual double standard turned marriage into a form of 'legalised prostitution'. Very much a product of Wollstonecraft's enthusiasm for the French Revolution, tempered by her disappointment at the failure to take up the cause of women's rights, the *Vindication* is at once optimistic, passionate and angry.

Appeal Of One-Half of the Human Race, Women, Against the Pretensions of the Other Half, Men, to retain them in Political and thence in Civil and Domestic Slavery by William Thompson (1825)

This pamphlet, whose wordy title is thankfully shortened to the *Appeal* in most discussions, was written in reply to James Mill's influential *Article on Government*. Mill had argued that neither women nor working class men needed the vote because women were looked after by men and working class men were looked after by their superiors. Thompson firmly refuted this argument by examining three common circumstances for women - wives, adult daughters who lived in their father's homes and women without fathers or husbands. Taking each group in turn, Thompson explored both their sexual and domestic oppression, comparing it to a form of slavery that could only end with complete legal equality. The *Appeal* emphasised the need for community childcare, access to education for girls, the opening up of all public office to women and an end to the sexual double standard. It aroused a good deal of debate and was one of the most important feminist documents of its time.

English Laws for Women in the Nineteenth Century by Caroline Norton (1854)

Ironically, Caroline Norton would have been appalled to find herself labelled as a feminist writer but *English Laws for Women* was extremely influential in bringing the plight of married women into the public arena. Once a woman married she lost the right to own property, to enter into legal contracts or to bring a case to court. In a nutshell, legally, married women only existed in relation to their husbands. When Caroline Norton returned to her violent husband after a short absence she found that he had removed her three sons and barred the house to her. Although her campaign to gain access to her children gained much support she met with no success. *English Laws for Women* highlighted Norton's tragic case and called for a reform of the law for married women. Despite her appalling treatment, Norton continued to accept the idea of male superiority, refusing to extend her appeal to include women's rights or sexual equality.

The Subjection of Women by John Stuart Mill (1869)

John Stuart Mill argued from the liberal point of view that sexual differences were the result of poor education coupled with legal and political inequalities. Once opportunities were opened up to women, he believed, these differences would be eroded. Women's oppression rested on custom and their education led them to expect an inferior position which in turn led to them becoming willing slaves. This was not helped by the fact that, as Mill admitted, boys were brought up to despise their mothers and sisters. Whilst Mill saw marriage as the 'normal' state and the care of the family as a woman's duty, *The Subjection of Women* was an indictment of nineteenth century marriage which he argued was degrading to both parties. He advocated a solution of equal rights in work, education, property and suffrage to restore the balance in marriage but largely ignored single women who made up a significant proportion of the population at that time.

The Morality of Marriage and Other Essays on the Status and Destiny of Women by Mona Caird (1897)

In its outspoken attack on marriage as a form of virtual enslavement of women, Mona Caird's collection of essays represents a significant contribution to the 'new woman' debate that was emerging in the late nineteenth century. Labelled as excessive and extreme by *The Woman's Sig-*

nal, one of two feminist journals which provided a platform for the debate, *The Morality of Marriage* elicited an appreciative correspondence from readers when it was serialised in the more radical journal, *Shafts,* with which Caird was closely associated. Ranked alongside Sarah Grand, Olive Schreiner and Elizabeth Robins as a 'new woman' novelist, Caird had already tackled the theme of marriage as institutionalised female slavery in her novel *The Daughters of Danaus* published in 1894, but it was her essays that added fuel to a debate that was already raging on the right of women to control their own lives.

A Room of One's Own by Virginia Woolf (1929)

A Room of One's Own was Virginia Woolf's contribution to the feminist debate. It documented the limited opportunities open to women writers because of their lack of financial independence. Woolf argued that without 'a room of one's own' and 'five hundred a year' women were denied the privacy and wherewithal to write well and freely. Calling upon historical precedents to support her argument, Woolf paid tribute to Aphra Behn, Jane Austen and the Brontës for their achievements despite the educational, social and financial disadvantages that they suffered. In her final chapter she discussed the idea of a harmonious 'androgyny' rather than rigidly defined 'male' and 'female' traits which, she argues, are unlikely to result in creativity. Together with its sequel, *Three Guineas*, published over ten years later, *A Room of One's Own* is now widely regarded as a classic of the feminist movement.

Other books by Virginia Woolf:

The Voyage Out (1915)

Night and Day (1919)

Jacob's Room (1922)

Mrs Dalloway (1925)

To the Lighthouse (1927)

Orlando (1928)

The Waves (1931)

The Years (1937)

Between the Acts (1941)

The Second Sex by Simone de Beauvoir (1953)

Considered to be one of the most important texts in the modern feminist canon, *The Second Sex* is a comprehensive study of the position of women in modern society and how they got there. Examining history, philosophy, economics, biology and literature, de Beauvoir concludes that women are not born into their position in society but that because society is constructed along patriarchal lines women are defined as 'other' than men and have become the 'second sex'. Banned by the Roman Catholic authorities when it was first published, *The Second Sex* is still a seminal text. The views expressed in the book on misogyny in myth and literature have been particularly influential. De Beauvoir's novels with their examination of the sexual hierarchy in relationships between men and women were also considered to be important feminist texts of the period.

The Feminine Mystique by Betty Friedan (1963)

The Feminine Mystique was said by many to be the book that gave the impetus to the resurgence of feminism in the sixties and seventies. A controversial best seller on publication, the book tapped in to the deep well of dissatisfaction that existed amongst those condemned to the boredom of housewifery. It grew out of a set of questionnaires that Friedan distributed amongst her college classmates into a polemic on the frustration of intelligent educated women drowning in middle class suburbia. Based on further questionnaires, interviews and discussions with psychologists, Friedan concluded that the pervasive feelings of worthlessness which afflicted her subjects resulted from a financial and emotional dependence on their husbands, coupled with an inability to find fulfilment in the role of wife and mother held up as the epitome of femininity.

Sexual Politics by Kate Millett (1969)

It was Kate Millet's *Sexual Politics* that set feminist literary criticism firmly on the academic agenda. Although primarily a work of scholarship with its origins in a PhD thesis, the book had such popular appeal that it became a best seller. Millett put forward the idea that whilst literature was a traditional means of expression for women it also reinforced their subordinate role through characterisation and language. Using D H Lawrence as a case study, Millett demonstrates her thesis by suggesting that Lawrence depicts women as the enemy, particularly in their role as independent wage-earner which had become a possibility in the early twentieth century. Millett's work owed a good deal to Simone de Beauvoir's *The Second*

Sex, an influence that, sadly, she seemed almost reluctant to acknowledge in her keenness to be seen as a trailblazer.

Other books by Kate Millett:
Flying (1976)
Sita (1977)
Elegy for Sita (1979)
The Loony Bin Trip (1991)
The Politics of Cruelty: An Essay on the Literature of Imprisonment (1994)

The Female Eunuch by Germaine Greer (1970)

Germaine Greer's clarion call to women to cast off their passivity, along with the stereotypes with which men kept them in their place, and celebrate their sexuality caused an immense stir when it was published in 1970 and is still quoted today. Greer argued that women had been 'castrated' both by themselves and by expectations built upon thousands of years of conditioning. As a result they demonstrated traits associated with eunuchs such as 'timidity, plumpness, languor, delicacy and preciosity'. An unashamed polemic for the sexual liberation of women, *The Female Eunuch* remains one of the classic texts associated with the resurgence of feminism during the late sixties and early seventies. Thirty years later, Greer wrote a sequel, *The Whole Woman*, in which she castigated the complacency of modern women telling them that it was 'time to get angry again'.

Our Bodies, Ourselves by The Boston Women's Health Collective (1973)

The Boston Women's Health Collective spearheaded the women's health movement with the publication of *Our Bodies, Ourselves*. In a world in which the medical profession was dominated by men, many of whom were perceived as unsympathetic or, worse, dismissive of women's health issues, this book encouraged women to get to know and understand their own bodies. As a result, should they need medical attention, they could seek it armed with the right information and a degree of confidence. The book was seen as radical by some people who disliked its explicit coverage of sexual issues, both heterosexual and gay, and its insistence on the importance of the politics of women's health. The original publishers, the non-profit-making Boston Women's Health Collective, have put together a new edition, *Our Bodies Ourselves for the New Century,* which includes information on websites and AIDS.

Hidden From History: Three Hundred Years of Women's Oppression and the Fight Against it by Sheila Rowbotham (1973)

In the seventies the feminist movement began to realise how important history was in demonstrating the injustices of the inequalities that women had endured for centuries. Sheila Rowbotham was one of the first to recognise the power of history as a tool for the movement. *Hidden from History* charts the influence of class, sex, work, family and social pressures on women's struggle to attain equality from the seventeenth century to the 1930s. In it, Row-

botham examined the effect of changes in working practises on both middle and working class women together
with the threat that improved contraception and the organisation of working women posed to the traditional male
control of the family. She argued that, for women, paid
work and work in the home are inextricably bound. With
its emphasis on historical context rather than individual
figures, *Hidden from History* initiated a new kind of feminist history.

Other books by Sheila Rowbotham:

Women's Consciousness, Man's World (1983)

The Past is Before Us: Feminists in Action Since the 1960s
(1989)

*A Century of Women: The History of Women in Britain and the
United States in the Twentieth Century* (1997)

Threads through Time: Writings on History and Autobiography
(1999)

Promise of a Dream: Remembering the Sixties (2000)

Fat is a Feminist Issue by Susie Orbach (1978)

Not to be mistaken for yet another self help book on
dieting, *Fat is A Feminist Issue* and its sequel *Fat is A
Feminist Issue II* were the first books to tackle the tyranny
of the scales in women's lives and to explore the reasons
behind that tyranny. Many women find themselves caught
up in a diet/binge trap, becoming obsessed with weight to
the point of developing disorders such as anorexia, bulimia
and compulsive eating. Arguing that the way in which
women's relegation to the role of wife and mother is inextricably bound up with their perception of their bodies,
Susie Orbach encouraged her readers to throw away their
calorie-counters and learn to accept themselves by under-

standing the social pressures upon them to attain the perfect body. A classic of its time, *Fat as a Feminist Issue* can be seen as a precursor to Naomi Wolf's *The Beauty Myth*.

Other books by Susie Orbach:

Fat is a Feminist Issue II (1982)

Outside In - Inside Out: Women's Psychology: A Feminist Psychoanalytical Approach (1982) with Luise Eichenbaum

What Do Women Want? (1983) with Luise Eichenbaum

Hunger Strike: The Anorectic's Struggle as a Metaphor for Our Age (1986)

Understanding Women (1992) with Luise Eichenbaum

The Impossibility of Sex (1999)

Towards Emotional Literacy (1999)

The Beauty Myth: How Images of Beauty Are Used Against Women by Naomi Wolf (1990)

In *The Beauty Myth* Naomi Wolf laid the blame for many of the ills that beset modern women firmly at the feet of those who create and perpetuate the idealised images which appear on advertising hoardings, in the pages of magazines and on television and cinema screens. From the workplace to the bedroom, Wolf argues that these images systematically oppress women, inhibiting both their confidence and the realisation of their potential. Citing the widespread occurrence of such problems as anorexia and poor self-esteem, Wolf suggests that the only way for women to escape the oppression of the 'beauty myth' is to step beyond it and see it for what it is - a means of making money and keeping women firmly in their place. *The Beauty Myth* took up some of the views expressed in Susie Orbach's *Fat is a Feminist Issue* and became one of the most influential feminist texts of the early nineties.

Other books by Naomi Wolf:

Fire with Fire: The New Female Power and How it Will Change the Twentieth Century (1993)

Promiscuities: The Secret Struggle for Womanhood (1997)

Backlash: The Undeclared War Against American Women by Susan Faludi (1991)

Feminists almost seemed to disappear in the eighties. Post-feminism started to be talked about as if everything was fine and dandy - all goals had been achieved. Susan Faludi's *Backlash* was a useful corrective to that idea. In her rigorously argued and lengthy study of the insidious attempts to undermine feminism she cites a Yale-Harvard research study with its conclusions that a women over thirty was more likely to be killed by a terrorist that to get married. The study received blanket media coverage in the States but as Faludi points out, its findings were likely to be dubious given its unreliable methodology. Faludi takes her readers through the many and various means which were employed during the Reagan-Bush era to try and put women back in their so-called place, from playing on the guilt of working mothers to the portrayal of women as vengeful viragos in films such as *Fatal Attraction*. Faludi followed the best selling *Backlash* with *Stiffed* (1999), an enquiry into the anger and discontent amongst American men that brought about the conditions for the backlash.

Feminist Novels

Listed below are just five feminist novels - a comprehensive list would require a book to itself. Women have a long tradition in literature from the plays of Aphra Behn to the understated feminism of Jane Austen with her quiet emphasis upon equality in marriage and education for women, to the more explicit messages in contemporary novels by authors such as Margaret Atwood. Feminist literary criticism began to be studied with the establishment of Women's Studies departments in many universities during the 1970s. It was at this time that the British publishing house Virago began reprinting feminist classics that had been unavailable for some time. For a detailed examination of feminist literature, try Lorna Sage's *Cambridge Guide to Women's Writing in English* (1999).

The Wanderer or Female Difficulties by Fanny Burney (1814)

Although Fanny Burney's status as a feminist author is disputed in some scholarly circles, claims that *The Wanderer* is a feminist novel can hardly be doubted with its theme of the difficulties inherent in being a woman in the eighteenth century. The heroine of *The Wanderer* is Juliet, a penniless émigré from revolutionary France trying to earn her living when opportunities for paid work were minimal. The opinions of her patroness and rival in love, Elinor Joddrel, are indisputably influenced by Mary Wollstonecraft, sentiments with which Juliet cannot agree. Maintaining its comic tone, the novel explores the new feminist views whilst graphically highlighting the plight of women. Written in the 1790s, it was not published until

1814 and, sadly, was the least successful of Burney's novels.

Other books by Fanny Burney:
Evelina (1778)
Cecilia (1782)
Camilla (1796)

The Yellow Wallpaper by Charlotte Perkins Gilman (1892)

First published in *The New England Magazine* as a short story, *The Yellow Wallpaper* is now often studied as a feminist text. This startlingly vivid first-person narrative tells of the descent into madness of a young woman after the birth of her first child. Isolated in her husband's large country mansion, her every material whim catered for but emotionally starved, the nameless woman tells us of her desperate need for intellectual stimulation. When her husband orders her to stay in her bedroom and pull herself together like a naughty child, her mind begins to unravel. *The Yellow Wallpaper* is made all the more poignant by the knowledge that Gilman suffered a mental breakdown, unable to cope with the stifling domestic routine that marriage inevitably brought in the late nineteenth century. She eventually divorced her husband and become an active feminist, lecturer and writer.

Other books by Charlotte Perkins Gilman:
Novels:
What Diantha Did (1910)
The Crux (1911)
Moving the Mountain (1912)
Herland (1915)

Non-Fiction:

In This Our World (1893)

Women and Economics (1898)

Concerning Children (1900)

The Home: Its Work and Influence (1903)

Man-Made World (1911)

The Golden Notebook by Doris Lessing (1962)

This long, complex and sometimes unwieldy novel was hailed as a landmark by the women's movement when it was first published. It centres on Anna, a young writer and single mother suffering from writer's block whilst trying to cope with crises in both her personal and political life. With a conventional narrative ironically headed 'Free Women' bracketing Anna's four experimental notebooks, the novel can, at times, be difficult to follow but its fragmentation is symbolic of the unravelling of Anna's life as she tries to keep each part of it separate from the rest. Anna suffers a breakdown which seems to release her from the chains that have bound her in her old life. Perhaps little read now, *The Golden Notebook,* together with Lessing's *Children of Violence* series, was one of the most important contributions to feminist fiction of the period.

A selection of books by Doris Lessing:

Novels

The Grass is Singing (1950)

Briefing for a Descent into Hell (1971)

Memoirs of a Survivor (1974)

The Good Terrorist (1985)

The Fifth (1988)

Love, Again (1996)

Mara and Dan, An Adventure (1999)

Ben, In the World (2000)

The Children of Violence Quintet:

Martha Quest (1952)

A Proper Marriage (1954)

A Ripple from the Storm (1958)

Landlocked (1965)

The Four-Gated City (1969)

Autobiography:

Under My Skin: Volume One of my Autobiography, to 1949 (1994)

Waiting in the Shade: Volume Two of my Autobiography 1949 to 1962 (1997)

The Women's Room by Marilyn French (1977)

In *The Women's Room*, Marilyn French charts the effect of the women's movement on ordinary suburban women's lives through the transformation of Mira Ward and her friends from 1950s housewives to 1970s feminists. Throughout the fifties and the sixties Mira attempts to stifle her own frustrations as she struggles to be a good wife and mother. Once the heady days of the seventies dawn, she begins to wake up to the possibilities of liberation. Her rebellion against the confines of her traditional marriage is exhilarating and stimulating although not without pain for both herself and her family. Although it has been criticised for its soap-opera style and would certainly be considered a period piece now, *The Women's Room* is nevertheless an accurate picture of the seismic upheavals going on in more than one household during the seventies.

Other books by Marilyn French:

Novels

Bleeding Heart (1980)

Her Mother's Daughter (1987)

Our Father (1994)

My Summer with George (1996)

Non-Fiction

Beyond Power: On Women, Men and Morals (1985)

The War Against Women (1992)

A Season in Hell (1998)

The Handmaid's Tale by Margaret Atwood (1985)

Many of Margaret Atwood's novels encompass feminist themes such as the relationship that women have with food in *The Edible Woman* or the sensational treatment of a murderess by newspapers in the nineteenth century in *Alias Grace*, but *The Handmaid's Tale* is generally considered to be her most explicitly feminist novel. Set in the Republic of Gilead sometime in the future, this is the story of the Handmaid Offred. Gilead is a nightmare world in which fertility has been so damaged that young woman such as Offred are kept as virtual prisoners, forced to copulate with the high-ranking official to whom they have been assigned. Once pregnant and safely delivered, they are venerated as symbols of womanhood although never set free. If they prove infertile or their pregnancies fail, they are banished to the Colonies as an Unwoman, forced to work in nuclear waste recycling plants. Atwood depicts a world so dominated by men that the Handmaids lose even their names - her feminist message is unmistakable.

Other novels by Margaret Atwood:

The Edible Woman (1969)

Surfacing (1972)

Lady Oracle (1976)

Life Before Man (1979)

Bodily Harm (1981)

Cat's Eye (1988)

The Robber Bride (1993)

Alias Grace (1996)

The Blind Assassin (2000)

Other Books of Interest

A History of Their Own: Women in Europe from Prehistory to the Present Volumes I and II by Bonnie S. Anderson and Judith P. Zinsser (Oxford University Press, 1988)

Testament of Youth by Vera Brittain (Virago, 1933)

English Feminism 1780- 1980 by Barbara Caine (Oxford University Press, 1997)

The Dialectic of Sex: The Case for Feminist Revolution by Shulamith Firestone (The Women's Press, 1979)

Significant Sisters: The Grassroots of Active Feminism by Margaret Forster (Penguin, 1986)

White, Male and Middle Class: Explorations in Feminism and History by Catherine Hall (Polity, 1992)

On Account of Sex: The Politics of Women's Issues, 1945 - 1968 by Cynthia Harrison (University of California Press, 1988)

Women in Public: The English Women's Movement, 1850 - 1900 by Patricia Hollis (Allen and Unwin, 1979)

The Spinster and her Enemies: Feminism and Sexuality, 1880 - 1930 by Sheila Jeffreys (Pandora, 1985)

Barbara Leigh Smith Bodichon and the Langham Place Circle edited by Candida Lacey (Routledge, Kegan and Paul, 1987)

Victorian Feminism, 1850 - 1900 by Philippa Levine (Hutchinson, 1987)

The Women's History of the World by Rosalind Miles (Harper-Collins, 1989)

Psychoanalysis and Feminism by Juliet Mitchell (Pelican, 1975)

Hyenas in Petticoats: A Look at Twenty Years of Feminism by Angela Neustatter (Penguin, 1989)

Who's Afraid of Feminism? Seeing Through the Backlash edited by Anne Oakley and Juliet Mitchell (Hamish Hamilton, 1997)

Housewife: High Value/Low Cost by Ann Oakley (Penguin, 1987)

Of Woman Born: Motherhood as Experience and Institution by Adrienne Rich (Virago Press, 1986)

The Origins of Modern Feminism: Women in Britain, France and the United States (1780 - 1860) by Jane Rendall (Macmillan, 1985,)

The Vintage Book of Feminism: The Essential Writings of the Contemporary Women's Movement edited by Miriam Schneir (Vintage, 1995)

Is the Future Female? Troubled Thoughts on Contemporary Feminism by Lynne Segal (Virago Press, 1987)

A Literature of Their Own: British Women Novelists from Charlotte Bronte to Doris Lessing by Elaine Showalter (Princeton University Press, 1977)

The Female Malady by Elaine Showalter (Virago Press, 1987)

There's Always been a Women's Movement This Century by Dale Spender (Penguin, 1984)

The Cause: A Short History of the Women's Movement in Great Britain by Ray Strachey (Virago Press, 1974 (1928))

Encyclopedia of Feminism by Lisa Tuttle (Longman, 1986)

Independent Women: Work and Community for Single Women, 1850-1920 by Martha Vicinus (Virago Press, 1985)

New Feminism by Natasha Walter (Virago Press, 1999)

Once a Feminist: Stories of a Generation by Michelene Wandor (Virago Press, 1990)

3. Key Figures In Feminism

Below are potted biographies of twenty key figures whose contribution to the women's movement has been vital. From Olympe de Gouges, who paid for her revolutionary demands for the equality of male and female rights with her life, to Germaine Greer, who both delighted and incensed many readers and commentators with her sassy intelligence in *The Female Eunuch*, each of the people listed below has made a difference to women's position in the world today.

Olympe de Gouges (1745 - 1793)

Olympe de Gouges' *Declaration of the Rights of Women and of the Citizen* (1791) was a great influence on Mary Wollstonecraft in her writing of *A Vindication of the Rights of Women* (1792).

The daughter of a butcher from Montauban in southern France, De Gouges, was married at sixteen to an older man. She was widowed shortly after the birth of her son and left Montauban for Paris where she changed her name from Marie Gouze and became an actress. By 1789, when the Revolution began, she was a recognised playwright and had begun writing pamphlets calling for reforms as diverse as the abolition of the slave trade, public workshops for the unemployed and a national theatre for women.

Her *Declaration* was written as a riposte to the revolutionary National Assembly's *Declaration of the Rights of Man and the Citizen* (1789) which had explicitly denied equal rights for women. De Gouges' reply sprang from a deep sense of frustration and betrayal shared by many other women who had taken an active part in the Revolution. Modelling her *Declaration* on the 1789 text and echoing its language she called for civil rights and citizenship to be extended to women because, she argued, that although women may be different from men, they were men's equals.

One of the rights claimed by de Gouges in her *Declaration* was the right to free speech. Sadly, this was denied her in the most brutal fashion. Her continued public assertions of the equality of women together with her association with the royalist Girondist faction, resulted in her arrest in July 1793. Later that year, she was sent to the guillotine.

French women were finally granted full citizenship in 1944.

Mary Wollstonecraft (1759 - 1797)

Mary Wollstonecraft is now widely accepted as the founder of modern Anglo-American feminism although she was not seen as such in her own time.

As the daughter of a less than wealthy farming family, she was well acquainted with the difficulties of making her own way in the world. In 1784 she managed to raise enough money to open a small school for girls at Newington Green in north London with her sister Eliza. Here she met a variety of radical Dissenters whose debates on the philosophical ideas of the Enlightenment stimulated her to write *Thoughts on the Education of Daughters* in 1786. By this time her school had become bankrupt and she was forced to take up a position as a governess in Ireland, one of the few respectable professions open to women of her class. In 1788 she returned to London and made her living by writing reviews and translations for the publisher, Joseph Johnson. In the same year Johnson published her first novel, *Mary*. During this time she became involved with Johnson's circle of friends, mixing with radicals such as William Godwin, Tom Paine and William Blake. In 1790 she wrote *A Vindication of the Rights of Man*, her reply to Edmund Burke's attack on the French Revolution, *Reflections on the Revolution in France* (1790). Disappointed by the revolutionaries' neglect of women's rights, Wollstonecraft's most famous work, *A Vindication of the Rights of Women*, followed two years later. In the same year she went to Paris, to see the revolution for herself, witnessing the execution of the king. Whilst there she began a passionate but short-lived relationship with Gilbert Imlay, an American writer. In 1794, she gave birth to Imlay's daughter, Fanny, publishing her observations on the French revolution in the same year. Despite her reputation as a firebrand, Wollstonecraft strongly believed in the importance of motherhood and was scathing about those who did not agree with her. On returning to London in 1795, Imlay's neglect led her to two suicide attempts. Two years later she married William Godwin but died from septicaemia shortly after the birth of their daughter, Mary, who grew up to become Mary Shelley, the author of *Frankenstein*.

Wollstonecraft is now heralded as a symbol of feminist revolt but, during her own time and for a considerable period after her death, feminists kept their distance from her, not wanting to be associated with her demands for the recognition of women's sexuality or the whiff of scandal that hung around her reputation.

Books by Mary Wollstonecraft:

Thoughts on the Education of Daughters (1787)

Mary (1788)

A Vindication of the Rights of Man (1790)

A Vindication of the Rights of Women (1792)

Books about Mary Wollstonecraft:

Memoirs of the Author of the Vindication of the Rights of Women by William Godwin (1798)

The Life and Death of Mary Wollstonecraft by Claire Tomalin (1974)

Mary Wollstonecraft by Janet Todd (2000)

Hannah More (1745 - 1833)

Hannah More would certainly not have described herself as a feminist, preferring to emphasise subordination, obedience, patience and humility as essential to a woman's good character. Nevertheless she did much to advance opportunities for women and deserves recognition for doing so.

Educated at her sister's boarding school in Bristol, More's literary aspirations were flattered by her inclusion in the Blue Stocking Circle, an informal discussion group that flourished in the late eighteenth century. Here she met Edmund Burke, Horace Walpole, Dr Johnson and Sir Joshua Reynolds. Horace Walpole admired her greatly, printing her play, *Bishop Bonner's Ghost* (1781), at his own printing press. She was also a friend of the celebrated actor David Garrick and his wife, with whom she lived for some time.

Her friendship with the abolitionist, William Wilberforce, brought her into contact with the Evangelical movement with which she was most impressed. Withdrawing from the distractions of London to her cottage in Somerset she wrote treatises such as *Thoughts on the Importance of the Manners of the Great to General Society* (1788), which emphasised traditional values. Such conservatism met with a warm reception at a time when news of the turmoil of the French Revolution was received with great anxiety.

In 1792, she published *Village Politics*, her reply to Thomas Paine's *Rights of Man* (1791-1792). It was a huge success and triggered a series of tracts that were circulated to the poor advising them on the virtues of sobriety, industry and trust in God. More was a strong believer in education but only up to a point. The poor were to be educated but must be reconciled to their fate. To that effect she set up women's clubs and schools for children which taught Bible studies, catechism and skills that she felt befitted their station.

More finally met with the literary success for which she had yearned with her novel *Coelebs in Search of a Wife* in 1809. She remained unmarried.

Although she accepted the sexual hierarchy More called for an educational system which would enable women to be moral guardians to their children, carry out their philanthropic duties and lay the foundations for a marriage based on friendship. Her pamphlet, *Strictures on the Modern System of Female Education* (1799), has recently attracted a good deal of interest from feminist historians and her contribution to feminism, albeit an unwitting one, should not be underestimated.

Books by Hannah More:

Strictures on the Modern System of Female Education (1799)
Coelebs in Search of a Wife (1809)

William Thompson (1785 - 1833)

Can men be feminists? Two of the most influential feminist texts of the nineteenth century were written by men - William Thompson's *Appeal Of One-Half of the Human Race, Women, Against the Pretensions of the Other Half, Men, to retain them in Political and thence in Civil and Domestic Slavery* (1825) and John Stuart Mill's *The Subjection of Women* (1869) - so some might argue that they can.

William Thompson, a wealthy Irish landlord with radical leanings, came to London in 1822 at the invitation of his friend, the philosopher Jeremy Bentham. Attracted by Bentham's 'greatest happiness for the greatest number' Utilitarian philosophy, Thompson eventually became involved in Robert Owen's more radical co-operative movement. Owen had succeeded in establishing several communities based on the ideas of equal opportunity and mutual co-operation which influenced the formation of the Trade Union and Socialist movements later in the century.

Thompson dedicated the *Appeal* to Anna Wheeler, a fellow Owenite, claiming that he was articulating her views. Some modern feminists give her more credit and describe her as co-writing the document. Wheeler, also from a wealthy Irish family, had been active for some time lecturing on women's rights. She divided her time between France, Ireland and England, translating French articles on female emancipation and socialism for the Owenite press.

Both Thompson and Wheeler were opposed to James Mill's argument that human nature inclines people to seek pleasure and power regardless of the effect on others. They took particular exception to his *Article on Government* which argued against universal enfranchisement. The *Appeal* was written in reply, focussing on the plight of women. It put forward the idea that women were trapped in 'artificial cages' constructed by men. When they married, they simply exchanged one cage for another. Arguing the Owenite view that marriage should be a co-operative relationship based on equality, Thompson declared the position of women to be tantamount to slavery. For both single and married women, equal rights enshrined in law were the only escape from this servitude.

The *Appeal* was undoubtedly one of the most influential feminist treatises of the early nineteenth century. So, perhaps men can be feminists after all, although, some might speculate as to why Wheeler was not given quite the credit she may have deserved.

Lucretia Mott (1793 - 1880)

Lucretia Mott was a pioneer of the American women's rights movement. In common with many suffrage campaigners, both American and British, she was an active abolitionist. In her work for the emancipation of slaves she must surely have drawn parallels with the plight of many women.

Born into a Quaker family, Mott grew up in Boston. When she was thirteen, she was sent to a Friends' boarding school near Poughkeepsie in New York State where she later became a teacher. Her discovery that she was paid only half the salary of her male colleagues kindled an interest in women's rights.

In 1811 she married a fellow teacher and moved to Philadelphia. She began addressing religious meetings in 1818, and was accepted as a minister of the Friends three years later. In the 1820s she travelled the country lecturing on religion, temperance and the abolition of slavery. She attended the founding convention of the American Anti-Slavery Society in 1833, setting up the Philadelphia Female Anti-Slavery Society as a result. In 1837 she helped organise the Anti-Slavery Convention of American Women, which met regularly in Pennsylvania Hall in Philadelphia. On May 16th, 1838, Mott calmly broke up a meeting when it became clear that an angry mob was at the door of the hall. Fortunately, although they burnt down the hall, the mob was diverted away from Mott's house.

Mott met fellow feminist, Elizabeth Cady Stanton at the World Anti-Slavery Convention in London in 1840. Women delegates were refused a seat at the convention and were subjected to the indignity of listening to the proceedings behind a curtain. Her treatment in London marked a turning point for Mott. She became more involved in campaigning for women's rights and, after several false starts, she and Stanton organised the first women's rights convention at Seneca Falls, New York in 1848. The convention issued a 'Declaration of Sentiments' modelled on the Declaration of Independence, stating, 'all men and women are created equal...'

Seneca Falls marked the beginning of the organised American women's movement and from 1848, Mott devoted most of her attention to women's rights, writing articles and lecturing widely. She was elected president of the 1852 convention at Syracuse and was also chosen president of the American Equal Rights Association at its inaugural meeting in 1866.

Since the passage of the Fugitive Slave Law in 1850, she and her husband had risked their lives by sheltering runaway slaves in their home. After the Civil War she worked for the enfranchisement of freed slaves and continued her work in the women's rights movement until her death.

A powerful orator, Mott remained calm before even the most hostile audiences. Her groundbreaking work both as a feminist and an abolitionist frequently put her in physical danger but her calm determination saw her through. Her contribution to the movement was invaluable.

John Stuart Mill (1806 - 1873)

John Stuart Mill was an eminent philosopher and economist. His work has had a profound influence on both nineteenth and twentieth century thinking and it is far beyond the scope of this book to give anything but the briefest of outlines of his achievements. His significance for our purposes lies in the publication of the highly influential *The Subjection of Women* in 1869 and his contribution to the campaign for equal rights.

Mill was born in London in 1806. Besides being a high-ranking official of the East India Company, his father, James Mill was also a philosopher and an economist. Mill was educated by his father with the advice and assistance of the Utilitarian philosopher, Jeremy Bentham. His education was intensive - he learned Greek at the age of three swiftly followed by Latin and a rigorous philosophical education. By the age of twenty, after suffering a breakdown, he turned to the writing of Coleridge, Wordsworth and Goethe for consolation. Throughout the remainder of his life, whilst advocating the necessity of a scientific approach to understanding social, political and economic issues, he also emphasised the importance of the arts.

He first put forward his ideas on the application of science to the social world in his *System of Logic* (1843) and his influential *Principles of Political Economy* was published in 1848. In 1859 his essay, *On Liberty*, unleashed a wave of controversy. In it he argued that the only restraint on liberty should be self-restraint - interference in another's liberty is only justifiable in self-defence.

In 1833 Mill met Harriet Taylor who was to heavily influence his thinking on women's rights. The two became close friends and colleagues, working together on many articles. They married in 1851 in the same year that their article the 'Enfranchisement of Women' appeared in the *Westminster Review*. Taylor died in 1854 but she undoubtedly influenced Mill in his writing of *The Subjection of Women*.

In the 1865 General Election, Mill stood as the Radical candidate for the Westminster seat. He campaigned for parliamentary reform alongside Henry Fawcett and in 1868 presented a petition in favour of women's suffrage organised by Barbara Bodichon, Emily Davies, Elizabeth Garrett and Dorothy Beale. Although he had succeeded in adding an amendment to the 1867 Reform Act, proposing equal political rights for men and women, it was defeated. In the same year he became one of the founding members of the London branch of the National Society for Women's Suffrage.

In 1869 Mill published *The Subjection of Women* which he had completed with the help of Harriet Taylor's daughter. In it he argued that, if freedom is good for men, it must also be good for women. He refuted the idea of differences between men and women as scientifically unproven, arguing that the only way to test the theory was to grant equal opportunities to men and women.

The Subjection of Women was extremely influential on the thinking of many suffrage campaigners, in particular Millicent Garrett Fawcett who became leader of the National Union of Women's Suffrage Societies. Mill's contribution to the issue of women's rights was significant and there can be little doubt that the respect accorded to his other work lent weight to his campaign for equality between the sexes.

Books by John Stuart Mill:

System of Logic (1843)

Principles of Political Economy (1848)

Thoughts on Parliamentary Reform (1859)

On Liberty (1859)

Considerations on Representative Government (1861)

Utilitarianism (1861)

The Subjection of Women (1869)

Autobiography (1873)

The Subjection of Women: Contemporary responses to John Stuart Mill edited and introduced by Andrew Pyle (1995)

Lucy Stone (1818 - 1893)

A prominent member of the women's suffrage movement, Lucy Stone also carried her feminist principles into her personal life, retaining her name when she married Henry B. Blackwell and omitting the word 'obey' from her wedding vows - common enough these days but revolutionary steps for the mid-nineteenth century.

Born into a poor Massachusetts farming family, Stone managed to save enough money to go to college when she was twenty-five. She chose Oberlin, Ohio, the first co-educational mixed-race American college, and graduated with honours in 1847. To pay for her tuition, she had to work as a domestic at the college.

After graduation, Stone became a lecturer for the Massachusetts Anti-Slavery Society and also began campaigning for women's rights. She toured the country lecturing, organising women's rights conventions, collecting signatures for petitions and addressing state legislatures whenever she could.

In May 1851 she met the abolitionist Henry B. Blackwell. At their wedding ceremony in 1855, they both read a protest 'against the present laws of marriage [which] refuse to recognise the wife as an independent, rational being'. Stone promised to love and honour her husband but not to obey him. She kept her own name and became known as Mrs Stone. In 1857, she gave birth to her only child, Alice Stone Blackwell.

Like her fellow suffrage campaigners, Stone worked for the Union cause during the Civil War which began in

1861. In 1863, she joined Susan B. Anthony and Elizabeth Cady Stanton in setting up the Woman's National Loyal League, in support of Lincoln's policies on the emancipation of slaves.

After the end of the war Stone supported Anthony's efforts to link the enfranchisement of the newly emancipated slaves with votes for women. The Fourteenth Amendment secured equal legal rights for all US born citizens but provoked bitter disappointment by using the word 'male' with regard to voting rights for the first time. The Fifteenth Amendment enfranchised black men but women's suffrage was not included. Stone supported the ratification of both Amendments whereas Anthony and Stanton opposed them, splitting the women's suffrage movement in 1869. The American Woman Suffrage Association campaigned for the vote on a state by state basis under Stone's leadership whilst Anthony and Stanton's National Woman Suffrage Association continued to fight for a Constitutional Amendment.

The two factions of the women's suffrage movement were not reconciled until 1890, largely through the efforts of Stone's daughter, Alice. Stone became chairman of the executive board of the newly formed National American Woman Suffrage Association with Stanton as its president.

Stone died at the age of 73 in 1893. In 1920, nearly three decades after her death, Congress adopted the Nineteenth Amendment, finally giving women throughout America the right to vote.

Susan B. Anthony (1820 - 1906)

One of the most important activists in gaining the vote for American women, Susan B. Anthony's concern for social reform sprang from her Quaker upbringing with its antipathy towards inequality. Her work in the temperance movement spurred her on to campaign for the rights of women, a decision that was crystallised when she met her fellow suffragist, Elizabeth Cady Stanton in 1851.

Born in New England, Anthony was educated at home until the age of seventeen when she began work as a teacher in New York. She joined the Daughters of Temperance in 1849 and began writing for *The Lily*, the first American newspaper to be owned by a woman. In 1851, Amelia Bloomer, the paper's editor, introduced Anthony to Elizabeth Cady Stanton who was to become her closest friend and colleague.

Anthony attended her first women's rights convention in Syracuse in 1852. She began to campaign for a change in women's property rights and in 1860 the New York state legislature passed the Married Women's Property Act allowing women to enter into contracts and control their own earnings and property.

Like many other suffragists, Anthony worked alongside the abolitionists during the Civil War, helping to form the Women's Loyal League in support of Abraham Lincoln's anti-slavery policies in 1863. After the war she attempted to link women's suffrage with the enfranchisement of freed slaves but without success. The Fifteenth Amendment gave the vote to black men but not to women, provoking much bitterness amongst suffragists.

In 1869, the women's suffrage movement split. Under Anthony and Stanton, the National Woman Suffrage Association continued to campaign for a Constitutional Amendment on enfranchisement whilst its rival, The American Woman Suffrage Association led by Lucy Stone, set about getting female suffrage adopted state by state.

In 1872, Anthony decided to challenge the Fourteenth Amendment of 1868 which had declared that all people born in the United States were citizens and that no citizen could be denied legal privileges but had introduced the word 'male' in connection with voting rights. Reasoning that women were citizens and the vote was a legal privilege, Anthony registered to vote in Rochester on November 1, 1872 and, with fifteen other women, voted in the presidential election. All sixteen were arrested but only Anthony appeared in court. Her trial began on June 17, 1873. Refusing to let Anthony testify, the judge ordered the jury to find her guilty, sentencing her to pay a $100 fine. Although she refused to pay, no further action was taken.

Between 1881 and 1886, Anthony and Stanton published three volumes of *The History of Woman Suffrage*. In 1890 both women's suffrage organisations were reconciled and merged to form The National American Woman Suffrage Association with Stanton as President and Anthony as Vice-President. When Stanton retired in 1892, Anthony took over as President until 1900 when, aged 80, she, too, retired.

Through Anthony's valiant efforts, many professions were open to women by the end of the nineteenth century. She was a tireless campaigner for women's suffrage, appearing before every Congress from 1869 until the year of her death. Sadly, only four states - Wyoming, Colorado, Idaho, and Utah - had given women the vote by the time she died.

In 1920 Congress adopted the Nineteenth Amendment, finally giving women throughout America the right to vote. In a touching tribute to Anthony's sterling efforts, the Nineteenth Amendment is more informally known as the Susan B. Anthony Amendment.

Josephine Butler (1828 - 1906)

The nineteenth century tradition of female philanthropy which grew out of the idea that women were natural moral educators allowed feminists such as Josephine Butler to campaign for women's rights without stepping too far outside the pale of middle class respectability. Butler played a major part in the repeal of The Contagious Diseases Acts which had virtually legalised brothels by placing prostitutes under police supervision in garrison towns and seaports, resulting in the legal enforcement of yet another variation on women's enslavement.

Butler was the daughter of Hannah Anett and her husband John Grey, a wealthy landowner and keen supporter of social reform.

In 1852 she married George Butler, an examiner of schools. The couple actively supported the anti-slavery movement and like many other feminists, Butler drew a parallel between the enslavement of Negroes and the enslavement of women.

In the first five years of her marriage, Butler had five children. It was the death of her daughter, Eva, in 1863 that led her to immerse herself in public life. The following year she became involved in a campaign to persuade Cambridge University to offer more opportunities for women students, resulting in the provision of lectures for women and the eventual establishment of Newnham College.

In 1868 she published *The Education and Employment of Women* in which she argued for improved educational and employment opportunities for single women. In the following year, she published *Women's Work, Women's Culture*. Butler believed that women were different from men but argued that enfranchisement would enable women to exercise their role as moral guardians more effectively.

In 1869 she became a founding member of the Ladies National Association for the Repeal of the Contagious Diseases Acts which was kick-started by Harriet Martineau. The Acts of 1864, 1866 and 1869 stated that medical examination of prostitutes in garrison towns or seaports should be enforced under police supervision. Diseased women were to be treated in a lock-up hospital. The government claimed that the Acts controlled the spread of venereal disease whilst ensuring that 'good' women went unmolested. Butler led the campaign for repeal, touring the country making powerful speeches that shocked an audience unprepared to hear a respectable middle class woman talking about sex. The campaign lasted more than sixteen years, finally succeeding with the repeal of the Acts in 1886.

Butler was also active in the campaign against child prostitution. Her part in exposing the case of Eliza Armstrong, who was 'bought' for £5 from her father by a woman working in a London brothel, helped to bring about the Criminal Law Amendment Act which raised the age of consent from thirteen to sixteen

Throughout her work, Butler was fully supported by her husband. When he became ill in 1886, she retired from public life to nurse him. After his death in 1890 she wrote her *Recollections of George Butler* (1892) and *Personal Reminiscences of a Great Crusade* (1896). Although too frail to take an active role, she became a supporter of the National Union of Suffrage Societies. She died on 30 December 1906.

Books by Josephine Butler:

The Education and Employment of Women (1868)

Women's Work, Women's Culture (1869)

Personal Reminiscences of a Great Crusade (1896)

Millicent Garrett Fawcett (1847 - 1928)

Millicent Garrett Fawcett worked for fifty years as a campaigner for women's suffrage, preferring a softly, softly approach to the more dramatic militant action of Emmeline Pankhurst's Women's Social and Political Union. Her name may not be as well known as Pankhurst's but there is no doubt that her quietly determined strategy played an important part in winning the vote for women.

Born in the Suffolk town of Aldeburgh in 1847, Fawcett was twelve when her sister, Elizabeth Garrett, moved to London and began her fight to qualify as a doctor.

Angered by her sister's struggle to gain entry to the medical profession despite her undoubted ability, Fawcett became determined to fight for women's rights. Her sister became the first woman to qualify as a doctor.

In 1865 Fawcett attended a speech on women's rights given by John Stuart Mill who became both a friend and a strong influence on her thinking. Through him she met many other feminist sympathisers including Henry Fawcett, MP for Brighton and professor of Economics at Cambridge. They were married in 1867 and had one child, Phillipa, born in 1868.

Fawcett helped her husband overcome his blindness in his work as an MP but was also politically active through her writing. She wrote many essays and books including *Political Economy for Beginners* (1870). Like Mill, she was an economic liberal who strongly supported the free market and viewed any state interference as an infringement of liberty.

She met many social reformers in Cambridge, working alongside Josephine Butler in the campaign to open the University to women that later evolved into Newnham College where her daughter was to become a student.

She served on the Married Women's Property Commission and became an active member of the London Suffrage Committee from 1868. An excellent organiser, she became a well-respected figure in the movement.

After her husband's death in 1884, Fawcett devoted herself to the National Union of Women's Suffrage Societies (NUWSS). She became leader of the NUWSS in 1897, campaigning for the enfranchisement of women whilst giving more militant suffrage organisations such as Emmeline Pankhurst's Women's Social and Political Union a very wide berth.

In July 1901 Fawcett was sent by the government to South Africa to investigate the British concentration camps which had been set up to contain Boer civilians during the war of 1899 to 1902. Her report, which vindicated the administration of the camps, has since been considered by many to be something of a whitewash.

Fawcett suspended the campaigning activities of the NUWSS when war broke out in 1914, returning to them when the war ended. In 1918, when women over the age of thirty were given the vote, Fawcett resigned as president of NUWSS but continued to campaign for equal franchise, equal opportunity in the professions and the reform of the divorce laws. In celebration of their victory, the NUWSS was renamed the National Union for Equal Citizenship under the leadership of Eleanor Rathbone.

Fawcett spent her later years travelling and writing. In 1925, she was made a Dame of the British Empire.

Fawcett's campaigning work for woman's suffrage spanned fifty years. Modern feminists may fight shy of her economic liberalism, with its Thatcherite connotations, but her contribution to the achievement of women's suffrage is undoubted. She died in 1929, one year after the franchise was fully extended to women.

Books by Millicent Garrett Fawcett:
Political Economy for Beginners (1870)

Women's Suffrage (1912)
Women's Victory and After (1918)
What I Remember (1924)
Josephine Butler (1927)

Emmeline Pankhurst (1858 - 1928)

Emmeline Pankhurst spent forty years as a militant campaigner for women's suffrage. In 1928, the year of her death, her dream became reality as the women of Britain were finally fully enfranchised. Both her daughters were active in the suffrage movement - Christabel, alongside her mother, whilst Sylvia preferred a more pragmatic approach.

The daughter of a Manchester manufacturer with radical sympathies, she married Richard Pankhurst in 1878. A supporter of women's rights, Richard Pankhurst was the author of the first British women's suffrage bill and of the Married Women's Property Acts (1870, 1882) which amended the laws preventing married women from owning their own property. He died, suddenly, in 1897.

In 1889 Pankhurst founded the Women's Franchise League which scored a small victory for women's suffrage by securing the right for married women to vote in local government elections. She went on to set up the Women's Social and Political Union (WSPU) in 1903.

On October 13 1905, Christabel Pankhurst and Annie Kenney were thrown out of a Liberal Party meeting for demanding a statement about the Party's stance on female suffrage. They were arrested in the street for spitting at a policeman and imprisoned when they refused to pay their fines. This caused quite a stir in a society unused to the idea of middle class women being dragged off to prison. From the outraged reaction to this event, both mother and daughter recognised the power of militant action.

In 1906 Pankhurst moved to London but continued to run the WSPU. The 1906 general election campaign offered plenty of scope for militant action. Suffragists persistently interrupted electoral meetings shouting, 'Votes for women' and demanding to know what was to be done about women's suffrage after the election.

From 1908-09 Pankhurst, now in her fiftieth year, was imprisoned three times. In 1911 she agreed to call off her campaign so as to ensure safety at the new King's coronation. In return, she was promised a bill enfranchising propertied women. When this was blocked, a wave of anger was unleashed amongst WSPU members who rampaged through the West End smashing windows. From July 1912 the campaign was stepped up, orchestrated by Christabel Pankhurst from Paris where she had gone to avoid conspiracy charges. Many women who were imprisoned went on hunger strike, resulting in shockingly violent force-feeding. Along with her supporters, Pankhurst found herself subject to the infamous 'Cat and Mouse Act' which resulted in hunger-striking prisoners being freed until they were well enough to be put back in gaol. She was released and re-arrested twelve times within one year.

When World War One broke out in 1914, she and Christabel called off the campaign and all suffragist prisoners were released. Supporters of the WSPU were encouraged to follow their leader's example and throw themselves into the war effort.

In 1917, women over thirty were awarded the vote. The Representation of the People Act, which finally established equal voting rights for men and women in 1928, was passed a few weeks before Pankhurst's death.

Although many women were involved in effective, if less dramatic, campaigns, Emmeline Pankhurst remains the name most associated with the achievement of women's suffrage in Great Britain.

Books about Emmeline Pankhurst:

My Own Story by Emmeline Pankhurst (1914)

Emmeline Pankhurst by Margaret Hudson (1998)

Clara Zetkin (1857 - 1933)

Clara Zetkin was an enthusiastic proposer of International Women's Day, which was first celebrated in Europe on March 19, 1911. Although it has had something of a sketchy history, International Women's Day was adopted by the United Nations in 1975 and is now recognised in most countries. It continues to provide a focus for women's rights campaigners.

Zetkin was born in Saxony in Germany. She was educated at the Leipzig Teachers' College for Women where she attended lectures by Wilhelm Liebknecht, founder of the newly formed *Sozialdemokratische Partei Deutschlands* (The German Social Democratic Party), which was later outlawed by Bismarck. She also met Ossip Zetkin, the Russian revolutionary whose name she adopted although they never married, joining him in exile in Paris. She spent most of the 1880s in Switzerland and Paris, writing and distributing dissident literature. During that time she met and worked with many leading Socialists.

In 1889, she was one of eight women delegates to the founding congress of the Second Socialist International. She returned to Germany in 1890 when the ban on the Social Democratic Party was lifted. From 1892 until 1917 she edited the Socialist women's paper *Die Gleichheit* (Equality). She helped to found the International Socialist Women's Congress in 1907 and was elected Secretary of the Women's Bureau.

In 1910, Zetkin put a proposal to the Congress that women throughout the world should focus on a particular day each year to publicise their demands. The conference of over one hundred women, representing unions, socialist parties and working women's clubs, greeted this suggestion with unanimous approval.

The first International Women's Day was held on March 19, 1911 in Germany, Austria, Denmark and a few other European countries. Women's suffrage campaigners distributed over a million leaflets throughout Germany, calling for action on women's right to vote. Many people, men and women, showed their support by marching through the streets.

March 8th was finally settled upon as a fixed date for International Women's Day. It was chosen in commemoration of the 1857 strike by hundreds of female textile workers in New York City in protest against appalling working conditions, exploitative wages and long working hours.

Zetkin was elected to the *Reichstag* in 1920 and served as a Communist until 1933 when, fearful of the consequences of Nazism, she fled to the Soviet Union. She died there in the same year.

Zetkin had fought hard for woman's suffrage to be included in the socialist programme. Her work to establish International Women's Day paid off and although it may sometimes be overlooked, feminists throughout the world still use it as a way of focussing their campaigns. German women finally won the vote in 1918.

Eleanor Rathbone (1878 - 1946)

Taking the baton from Millicent Garrett Fawcett in 1919, Eleanor Rathbone led the National Union of Societies for Equal Citizenship (NUSEC) to victory with the passage of the Equal Franchise Act in 1928 which finally gave British women equal voting rights with men. Her other area of outstanding achievement was her work on family economics, widely considered to be the greatest influence in the introduction of the Family Allowance which gave mothers a small measure of financial independence.

Rathbone was the daughter of one of Liverpool's best-known philanthropic Quaker families. Her father, William Rathbone, was the Liberal MP for the city. She was brought up in both Liverpool and London, going on to read Classics at Somerville College, Oxford.

When she returned to Liverpool in 1896, she became secretary of the Liverpool Women's Industrial Council. Her work in this area led her to understand the importance of financial independence and the link between wage earning and citizenship. In 1909, the year in which she became the first woman member of Liverpool City Council, she published her first book on family economics, *How the Casual Labourer Lives*. Together with women's suffrage, with which she had become involved in 1897 as a speaker for her local suffrage society, this was to become her main area of interest.

During the 1914 -1918 war, Rathbone worked in benefit administration and in 1918 her Family Endowment Committee published its pamphlet *Equal Pay and the Family*.

In 1919 she succeeded Millicent Garrett Fawcett as President of the National Union of Societies for Equal Citizenship whose name had been changed from the National Union of Women's Suffrage Societies in celebration of the Representation of the People Act 1917 which gave women over thirty the vote. She remained as president until equal voting rights with men were finally introduced in 1928.

In 1922 she stood unsuccessfully as an independent parliamentary candidate for East Toxteth but eventually succeeded in becoming an independent MP for the Combined English Universities. Once there, she raised questions in Parliament on women's issues including the plight of women in India. During World War II she worked with refugees in Europe.

Although she had taken up many social issues, Rathbone's main area of interest continued to be family economics. Her *Case for Family Allowances (1940)* heavily influenced the Family Allowance Act, which came into force in 1945, one year before her death. Thanks largely to her, those mothers who had previously been entirely dependent on men now had a small measure of financial independence.

Rathbone bridged the gap between nineteenth and twentieth century feminism. Women's suffrage loomed large in the nineteenth century but once the vote had been won it became clear that there was much more to done in the battle for equality with men. Her position as an MP gave Rathbone a degree of influence in making sure that her work on family economics was translated into legislation.

Books by Eleanor Rathbone:
How the Casual Labourer Lives (1909)
The Disinherited Family (1924)
The Case for the Family Allowance (1940)
Books about Eleanor Rathbone:
Eleanor Rathbone by Johanna Alberti (Sage, 1996)

Simone de Beauvoir (1908 - 1986)

Simone de Beauvoir's best-known book, *The Second Sex* (1949*)*, remains a seminal feminist text. It is a comprehensive and scholarly survey of the many influences that have relegated women to a position as the 'second sex' in society.

The daughter of a strict Roman Catholic middle class French family, de Beauvoir was privately educated and went on to graduate in philosophy from the Sorbonne in 1929. It was there that she met Jean-Paul Sartre with whom she had a lifelong relationship both as his colleague and his lover. Despite the best efforts of her deeply conservative family she established an independent life for herself in Paris. She taught in schools from 1931 to 1943 then turned to writing, setting up the monthly review, *Les Temps Modernes*, with Sartre in 1945 as a platform for the newly emerging philosophy of existentialism.

De Beauvoir's first published work was fiction. She wrote several novels which explored both existentialist and feminist views of modern life. In particular, *She Came to Stay* (1943), dissects the effects on the relationship between a man and a woman when a young and beautiful girl comes to live with them.

In the early fifties, commonly thought of as a fallow period for feminism, *The Second Sex* shone like a beacon. In this long and scholarly book de Beauvoir developed her ideas of a patriarchal society in which men see women as not just 'other' but 'secondary' to themselves. Exploring a multitude of disciplines from literature to biology, economics to philosophy, de Beauvoir documented the evolution of this patriarchy over centuries. She concluded with a passionate plea that women could only attain equality with men when their identity became independent of sexuality.

Aside from *The Second Sex*, de Beauvoir is perhaps best known for the four volumes of her autobiography which chronicle a life lived at the heart of French intellectual life from the 1930s to the 1970s. She also produced four volumes of philosophy, two travel books (one on China, the other on America) and many essays. In 1964, prompted by the death of her mother, de Beauvoir turned her attention to ageing. She wrote *A Very Easy Death* on the subject and went on to castigate society for its negligent attitude to the elderly in *Old Age* (1970).

Although de Beauvoir can hardly be described as an activist in the women's movement, both in her personal and in her professional life she lived according to the premise of *The Second Sex*, striving to find equality with her male peers independent of her sexuality.

Books by Simone de Beauvoir

The Second Sex (1949)

A Very Easy Death (1964)

Old Age (1970)

Fiction

She Came to Stay (1943)

The Mandarins (1954)

The Woman Destroyed (1969)

Autobiography

Memoirs of a Dutiful Daughter (1958)

The Prime of Life (1960)

Force of Circumstance (1963)

All Said and Done (1972)

Adieux: Farewell to Sartre (1981)

Books about Simone de Beauvoir:

Simone de Beauvoir by Deirdre Bair (1990)

Simone de Beauvoir: A Critical Reader by Elizabeth Fallaze (Editor), Routledge (1998)

De Beauvoir and the Second Sex: Feminism, Race and the Origins of Existentialism by Margaret A. Simons (1999)

Betty Friedan (1921 -)

Betty Friedan is perhaps best known as the author of *The Feminine Mystique* published in 1963. Often said to have triggered the formation of the women's movement in the sixties and seventies, the book explores the frustrations endured by women in the fifties, stuck in the idealised role of wife and mother in which they were expected to find fulfilment.

Graduating from Smith College in 1942 with a degree in psychology, Friedan went on to do a year's postgraduate work at the University of California in Berkley before moving to New York City. In 1947 she married Carl Friedan and spent the next ten years living in the New York suburbs, writing occasional freelance articles for magazines but primarily working as a housewife and mother. In 1957, unsettled by her frustrations, she circulated a questionnaire amongst her old college friends. The results, which chimed with her own lack of fulfilment as a dependent housewife and mother, spurred Friedan on to further research which she published as *The Feminine Mystique* in 1963. The book unleashed a tidal wave of dissatisfaction from women like her, educated but frustrated by the limitations of their role.

Friedan formed the National Organisation for Women (NOW) in 1966. She had recently covered a conference on equal opportunity in employment at which women's issues had been sidelined and NOW's declared aim was the pursuit of equal opportunities for women. With Friedan's journalistic contacts in the media and political lobbies, NOW's campaigns on discriminatory employment practises, increased representation for women in government, the introduction of state childcare for working mothers and, most controversially, legalised abortion, met with a great deal of publicity. NOW remained the largest and most influential organisation in the American women's movement for many years. In 1970, Friedan stood down as president but continued to be an active member of the group. She helped organise the Women's Strike for Equality on August 26th 1970, the fiftieth anniversary of American women's suffrage. She was a founding member of the National Women's Political Caucus in 1971 and became director of The First Women's Bank and Trust Company in 1973.

In 1981 she published *The Second Stage* in which she assessed the achievements of the women's movement so far. *The Fountain of Age* (1993) published when she was seventy-two confronted society's contemptuous attitude towards old age in the same feisty manner that characterises all of Friedan's writing.

Books by Betty Friedan:
The Feminine Mystique (1963)
It Changed My Life: Writings on the Women's Movement (1976)
The Second Stage (1981)
The Fountain of Age (1993)
Life So Far (2000)

Gloria Steinem (1934 -)

Perhaps better known in the United States than in Great Britain, Gloria Steinem is regarded as one of the most outspoken and articulate figures of the seventies women's movement. In 1971 she set up *Ms.*, a widely respected magazine which examined social issues from a feminist perspective. It sold in huge numbers and, thirty years later, Steinem still remains associated with it. It was Steinem who coined one of the best-known feminist catchphrases of the seventies – 'a woman needs a man like a fish needs a bicycle'.

Steinem spent her earliest years on the road with her parents. When they divorced in 1946 she and her mother settled in Toledo, Ohio. Much of her childhood was spent trying to cope with her mother's chronic depression and eventually she moved to Washington D.C. to live with her older sister. She won a scholarship to the prestigious Smith College and graduated with honours in 1956, something of an achievement for someone whose regular schooling had only started ten years before.

A two-year fellowship took her to India to study at Delhi and Calcutta Universities. Here she became involved with non-violent protest against government policy in the bitterly divided southern region of the country. Exposed to extremes of poverty, she became deeply politicised by her experiences in India.

In 1960, she began working as a writer and journalist in New York City. Two years later she made the headlines with her article '*I Was a Playboy Bunny*', which told the story of her experience as a scantily clad waitress at Hugh Hefner's Playboy Club, exposing its poor wages and working conditions.

By 1968 Steinem's work had become more obviously political, addressing many liberal issues in her '*The City Politic*' column for *New York* magazine. After she went to a meeting of the radical feminist group, the Redstockings, in 1968 she threw herself into the newly emerging women's liberation movement, becoming a passionate and articulate activist. Along with Betty Friedan, she was a founding member of the National Women's Political Caucus in July 1971 which was set up to encourage women to become actively involved in the 1972 presidential election. Steinem argued for a positive policy on abortion to be included in the Democrat manifesto.

That same year she set up *Ms.,* a magazine that gave a feminist slant to many contemporary issues. The first issue was a sell-out. Steinem is still associated with her trailblazing magazine.

Steinem has long been a Democrat supporter and has also been involved with a number of political organisations including the Coalition of Labour Women, Voters for Choice, and Women Against Pornography.

She remains an ardent and articulate supporter of women's rights.

Books by Gloria Steinem:

Outrageous Acts and Everyday Rebellions (1983)

Marilyn (1986)

Revolution from Within (1992)

Moving Beyond Words (1994)

Books about Gloria Steinem:

Education of a Woman: The Life of Gloria Steinem by Carolyn Heilbrun (Virago, 1997)

Germaine Greer (1939 -)

Germaine Greer's name became almost synonymous with the word 'feminist' after the publication of *The Female Eunuch* in 1970. With her forthright views, her open sexuality and her quick wit, she was a gift to the media who either labelled her as a strident, if sexy, bra-burner or lauded her as the high priestess of the women's movement.

Born in Melbourne, Australia, Greer first came to Britain to study for her doctorate in literature at Cambridge University. After leaving Cambridge she did a little acting, wrote for a variety of journals and lectured at Warwick University. In 1970 *The Female Eunuch* exploded onto the feminist scene. Although it was a serious analysis of female stereotypes as a form of male oppression, Greer's exhortations to women to get to know their bodies and seek out sexual satisfaction rather than lying on their backs and thinking of England, meant that she found herself both taken seriously and lampooned mercilessly. It became the book that every self-respecting, left-leaning woman had on her bookshelves or by her bed.

Over time her views changed to a degree and, once again, she found herself the target of criticism. In *Sex and Destiny* (1984), she suggested that sexual liberation may have a downside for women's fertility and was accused of reneging on her original ideas.

Like Betty Friedan and Simone de Beauvoir, Greer turned her attention to society's attitudes towards ageing women in *The Change* (1991). Urging women to take responsibility for health issues into their own hands, she went on to explore the stereotypes of the ageing woman concluding that they are a male fabrication.

In 1999, thirty years after the publication of *The Female Eunuch*, Greer was moved to write a sequel despite her many protestations that she would never do so. Starting the book with the statement that 'it's time to get angry again', Greer went on to review the achievements of the past thirty years and find them lacking. She lambasted young women for accepting the idea that the battle was won, citing examples such as the perfection of plastic surgery techniques on women's breasts whilst breast cancer continued to go undetected and uncured.

Forthright, intelligent, articulate and unafraid, Greer remains a voice to be listened to.

Books by Germaine Greer:

The Obstacle Race: The Fortunes of Women Painters and Their Work (1979)

Sex and Destiny: The Politics of Human Fertility (1984)

The Madwoman's Underclothes: Essays and Occasional Writings (1986)

The Change: Women, Ageing and the Menopause (1991)

The Whole Woman (1999)

Andrea Dworkin (1946 -)

As a radical lesbian, Andrea Dworkin belongs to one of the more extreme forms of feminism. In the seventies and the eighties she was frequently associated with the sort of vitriolic attacks on feminism by the media which had so many women saying 'I'm not a feminist but..' before going on to demonstrate that they were.

Dworkin was born in Camden, New Jersey in 1946. As an undergraduate at Bennington College in Vermont, she became involved in anti-Vietnam War demonstrations. After one such protest, she was arrested and held at the New York Women's House of Detention. The treatment she received there led her to begin the formulation of her ideas on the way that men exert control over women.

In 1974, Dworkin published her first book, *Women Hating: A Radical Look at Sexuality*, in which she attacked pornography, linking it with violence against women. Together with feminist lawyer, Catherine A MacKinnon, she continued her polemic with *Pornography and Civil Rights: A New Day for Women's Equality* (1988). They had already drafted a controversial ordinance that, by classifying pornography as a form of sex discrimination, would allow those who felt victimised to sue the makers and distributors of pornography. Dworkin and MacKinnon were successful in getting the feasibility of their ordinance debated in several cities beginning with Minneapolis in 1982. Although the city passed the ordinance on two separate occasions, the mayor twice vetoed it. Three other cities held hearings - Indianapolis in 1984, Los Angeles in 1985 and Boston in 1992 but did not enact the ordinance.

Dworkin continues to write essays, books and give speeches on the links between pornography and violence towards women, from child abuse to male coercion of women into prostitution.

Books by Andrea Dworkin:

Woman Hating: A Radical Look at Sexuality (1974)

Pornography: Men Possessing Women (1981)

Our Blood: Prophecies and Discourses in Sexual Politics (1982)

Right-wing Women: The Politics of Domesticated Females (1983)

Life and Death (1987)

Intercourse (1987)

Letters from the War Zone: Writings 1976 - 1987 (1988)

Scapegoat: The Jews, Israel and Women's Liberation (2000)

Fiction

Ice and Fire (1986)

Mercy (1991)

Susan Faludi (1959 -)

Susan Faludi is best known for her book *Backlash: The Undeclared War Against Women* (1991), an exhaustively researched and rigorously argued study of the way in which the media has consistently attempted to undermine the advances made by women in the late twentieth century. One of the most influential feminist books to be published during the nineties, *Backlash* provoked a storm of controversy when it appeared.

Faludi's journalistic career began as managing editor of *Harvard Crimson* when she was an undergraduate in the early eighties. She frequently wrote about women's issues including the incidence of sexual harassment at Harvard. As soon as she graduated she found her way into journalism, starting at the bottom as a copy clerk for *The New York Times*. She went on to become a reporter for *The Miami Herald*, followed by the *Atlanta Constitution*, and the *San Jose Mercury News*. In 1990 she joined the San Francisco office of *The Wall Street Journal*, winning a Pulitzer Prize for journalism in 1991. *Backlash* was published in the same year and received enormous attention for its attack on the media's negative portrayal of modern women from both sides of the argument. She won a National Book Critics Circle Award for general non-fiction with the book in 1992.

Faludi went on to write *Stiffed: The Betrayal of the American Man*, an equally well-researched investigation into the frustration and anger of American working-class men and the influence of that anger on their attitudes towards women.

Books by Susan Faludi:
Backlash: The Undeclared War Against Women (1991)
Stiffed: The Betrayal of the American Man (1999)

Greenham Common Women (1981 - 2000)

Not a single figure but a large body of women who chose to exclude men from their resistance to the male dominated nuclear arms industry.

On the 28th of August 1981 a group of women marched 110 miles from Cardiff in Wales to Greenham Common in Berkshire. They were protesting against the NATO decision to site Cruise Missiles at RAF Greenham Common which had become a base for the United States Airforce. The women set up the Peace Camp outside the main gate of the base which became known as Yellow Gate when other satellite camps sprung up around the nine-mile perimeter fence of the base.

The camps attracted thousands of women from all over the world and from all walks of life. They took part in many non-violent protests from individual acts such as cutting the wire perimeter fences to the 'Embrace the Base' demonstration when up to 30,000 women held hands around the nine-mile perimeter. The women were often treated roughly at the regular evictions from the camp but remained undeterred. They were vilified by the press who depicted them as man hating, jack- booted, ugly and, worst of all, feminists.

What started as a handful of people became a non-hierarchical community that was an inspiration for many women. The last caravan left on September 8th, 2000.

Greenham Common Women's Peace Camp: A History of Non-Violent Resistance, 1984 - 1995 by Beth Junor (Working Press, 1995)

The Essential Library

New This Month:

Steven Spielberg (£3.99)   **Feminism** (£3.99)
Sherlock Holmes (£3.99)   **Alchemists & Alchemy** (£3.99)

Film Directors:

Woody Allen (£3.99)   **Jane Campion** (£2.99)
John Carpenter (£3.99)   **Jackie Chan** (£2.99)
Joel & Ethan Coen (£2.99)   **David Cronenberg** (£3.99)
Terry Gilliam (£2.99)   **Alfred Hitchcock** (£2.99)
Krzysztof Kieslowski (£2.99) **Stanley Kubrick** (£2.99)
Sergio Leone (£3.99)   **David Lynch** (£3.99)
Brian De Palma (£2.99)   **Sam Peckinpah** (£2.99)

Ridley Scott (£3.99)   **Orson Welles** (£2.99)
Billy Wilder (£3.99)

Film Genres:

Film Noir (£3.99)   **Heroic Bloodshed** (£2.99)
Horror Films (£3.99)   **Slasher Movies** (£3.99)
Spaghetti Westerns (£3.99)   **Vampire Films** (£2.99)

Miscellaneous Film Subjects:

Steve McQueen (£2.99)   **Marilyn Monroe** (£3.99)
The Oscars® (£3.99)   **Filming On A Microbudget** (£3.99)

TV:

Doctor Who (£3.99)

Books:

Cyberpunk (£3.99)   **Philip K Dick** (£3.99)
Hitchhiker's Guide (£3.99)   **Noir Fiction** (£2.99)
Terry Pratchett (£3.99)

Ideas:

Conspiracy Theories (£3.99)   **Nietzsche** (£3.99)

Available at all good bookstores, or send a cheque to: **Pocket Essentials (Dept FE), 18 Coleswood Rd, Harpenden, Herts, AL5 1EQ, UK**. Please make cheques payable to 'Oldcastle Books.' Add 50p postage & packing for each book in the UK and £1 elsewhere.

US customers can send $6.95 plus $1.95 postage & packing for each book to: **Trafalgar Square Publishing, PO Box 257, Howe Hill Road, North Pomfret, Vermont 05053, USA**. e-mail: tsquare@sover.net

Customers worldwide can order online at **www.pocketessentials.com**.